AROUND WHITEHAVEN IN OLD PHOTOGRAPHS

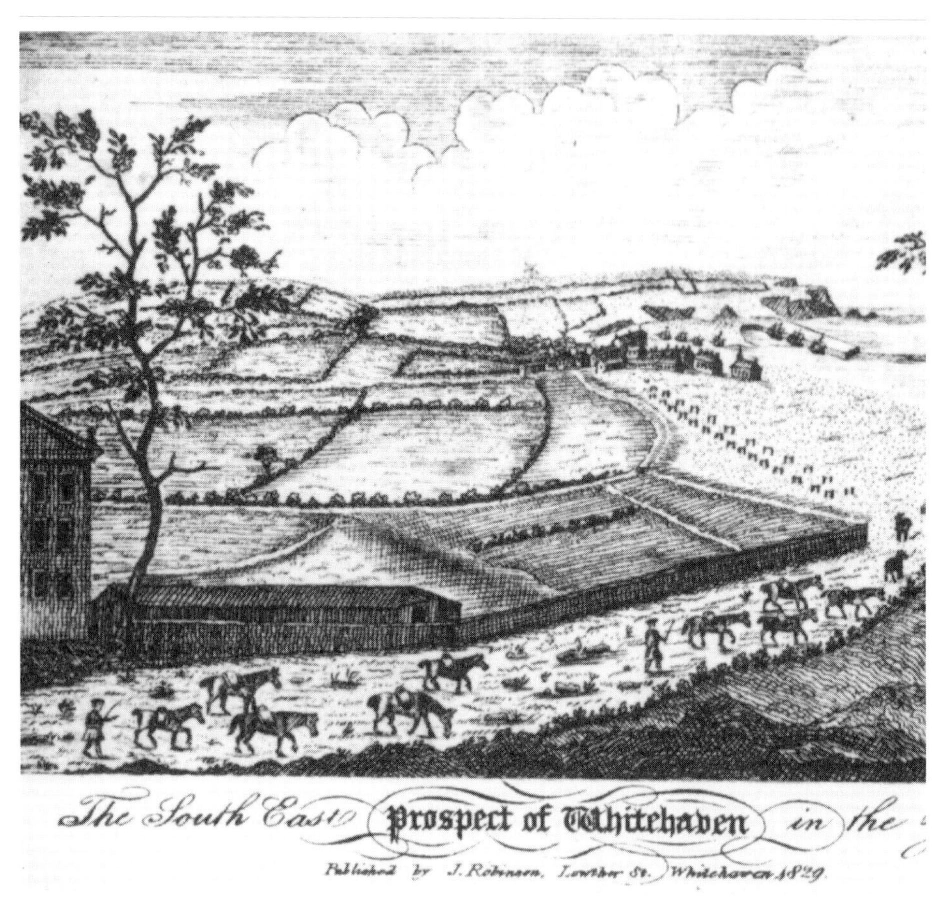

'A PROSPECT OF WHITEHAVEN, 1642,' published 1829. This view has an interesting history. The original pencil drawing was made by David King in 1642. About a century later the drawing was produced as an engraving, but in 1829 a tiny postcard-sized lithograph was published by J. Robinson of Lowther Street, Whitehaven as a form of advertisement. He claimed to be the first local printer to use the lithographic process and the card was used to demonstrate its possibilities. At the time of King's original drawing, Whitehaven was still a small village, but its period of rapid expansion was already under way. Within a century it was to develop into a major international port.

AROUND WHITEHAVEN IN OLD PHOTOGRAPHS

FROM THE PHOTOGRAPHIC ARCHIVES OF WHITEHAVEN MUSEUM

COMPILED BY
HARRY FANCY

ALAN SUTTON

Alan Sutton Publishing Limited
Phoenix Mill · Far Thrupp · Stroud · Gloucestershire

First published 1992

British Library Cataloguing in Publication Data

Fancy, Harry
Around Whitehaven in Old Photographs
I. Title
942.784

ISBN 0-7509-0113-6

Front Cover Illustration: RIGGERS at work on the *Thirlmere.*

Typeset in 9/10 Sabon.
Typesetting and origination by
Alan Sutton Publishing Limited.
Printed in Great Britain by
The Bath Press, Avon.

CONTENTS

INTRODUCTION

An official survey in 1566 of Britain's ports, creeks and harbours dismissed Whitehaven as six fishermen's cottages with a single nine-ton vessel, the *Bee*. The commissioners could have had no inkling that this insignificant bay was destined to become one of the leading ports of the British Isles. This remarkable transformation was brought about by the vision, determination and business acumen of three generations of the ancient Lowther family, whose roots can be traced to pre-Norman times. Their direct responsibility for the Whitehaven estate lasted from 1600 to 1755, from its earliest expansion to the peak of its prosperity.

Following the Dissolution of the Monasteries (1536–9), the confiscated lands of the adjacent Priory of St Bees passed through several hands until acquired by the Lowther family in 1600. It was not until 1634 that Christopher Lowther took up residence in the town and began its carefully planned development. Knowing that his lands contained seams of coal, and that this would find a ready market in the fast-growing city of Dublin, he at once started to construct a pier to give protection and moorings to collier vessels. Although subsequently lengthened, 'Old Quay' still stands. Over the centuries, many additional quays were built, culminating in the great 'lobster claws' of West and North Piers which extend defiantly into the Solway.

The Cumbrian coalfield is relatively small, covering some 100 square miles, much of this below the Solway estuary. The coal is of good quality, and several workable seams occur, the main or Prior band being from eight to as much as twelve or thirteen feet in thickness. Owing to the hilly nature of the area and subsequent erosion by glaciers and rivers, the upper coal measures outcrop at the surface, and could be mined by driving 'walk-in' passages into the hillside. As the most accessible seams were gradually worked out, it became necessary to drive ever-deeper shafts to reach new measures and, by the 1730s, Whitehaven possessed the deepest mines in the world. The Lowthers' intention was to establish a monopoly of the Irish coal trade. This they failed to achieve, as other landowners, including the Curwens, Moresbys and Fletchers, followed their example and developed rival harbours at Workington, Maryport, Harrington and Parton. The Lowthers, however, obtained the lion's share of the coal trade, due to their investment in the best available technology, their fiercely acquisitive land policy, and their role in Parliament.

In order to accomplish their aims, manpower was the first requirement. Men were needed to win the coal, transport it to the harbour, and build and sail the ships. These workers had to be housed and fed, and provided with shops, churches and public houses. Builders, brickmakers, quarrymen, carpenters, chandlers and tradesmen were required. These in turn required housing. There could be no half measures; once the scheme was embarked upon, a rapid build-up of population was inevitable. Once started, the process was self-generating, and must have appeared limitless as Dublin's demand for coal seemed insatiable. To permit yet regulate this mushroom growth, the Lowthers laid out a grid-like street pattern, allocated regular plots, and stipulated basic building requirements, insisting, for example, that all buildings must be three storeys in height. In so doing, they created the first planned town since medieval times, and its pattern remains virtually unchanged to this day.

Christopher Lowther initiated this spectacular growth, but he died at the age of 33 in 1644, having become the first Baronet of Whitehaven. His son John, then aged one and a half, inherited the title, but the estate was managed on his behalf by trustees until he reached the age of 21 years. Afterwards, he entered Parliament as Member for Cumberland. He was to remain an MP almost without break for over thirty years, and from 1689 to 1696 he served as one of the seven Lord Commissioners of the Admiralty at a salary of £1,000 per year. Apart from annual visits when Parliament was in recess, and for the last few years of his life, Sir John was an absentee landlord. His estate was supervised by carefully chosen stewards – shrewd, sometimes brilliant men in their own right – yet there can be no question that Sir John decided all major issues. His voluminous correspondence with the stewards has been preserved, so providing one of the most detailed accounts of the development of any British town of the period. On his death in 1706 his second son James took charge of the estate and the pattern was repeated, Sir James serving as an MP for fifty-five years. He, too, governed the estate through the medium of his stewards. Father and son worked incessantly in Parliament to protect the interests of Cumberland in general and Whitehaven in particular. They kept themselves abreast of the latest developments in trade, technology and science, and applied this knowledge to the further development of the town. This enlightened self-interest led to the acquisition of vast personal wealth, Sir James being described as 'the richest commoner in the land' by the time of his death in 1755. The last Baronet of Whitehaven, he died a bachelor, so the estate passed to another branch of the family. The Lowthers retained their control of the town until early this century, but were never again to exercise the same direct interest or control over its activities. It is a strange fact that during the century and a half of direct supervision of the estate by Christopher, John and James Lowther, the three men actually lived in the town they had created for a total of no more than twenty-five years.

During the late eighteenth century, a significant new factor entered the local economy in the form of trade links with the New World. Around 1675 entrepreneurs began to import tobacco from the Virginia area, exchanging this for mixed cargoes which would be of use to the colonists. During the winter every available ship was needed for the Irish coal trade, but as the season grew warmer the demand slackened, leading to surplus shipping capacity at the time of year most suitable for transatlantic voyages. For almost a century many of Whitehaven's collier brigs, little ships of 150–250 tons, engaged in this lucrative trade. They also established an important Caribbean trade, importing mainly sugar and spirits. Several merchants acquired estates in the New World, and trading stations were set up to facilitate the exchange of cargoes. A small number of merchants also entered the slave trade, but this never became a significant factor. Around 1760, for complex reasons, Whitehaven's tobacco trade failed and several leading merchants became bankrupt, among them William Younger.

One of his apprentice seamen at the time was a youth called John Paul who was born at Kirkbean, a small village on the Scottish side of the Solway. Younger obtained for him the post of third mate aboard a slave ship, the second of only two such vessels ever built at Whitehaven.

So John Paul sailed from Whitehaven on the maiden voyage of the *King George* in 1763. Fifteen years later, after an adventurous career and having added the name 'Jones' to his own, he returned to Whitehaven as commander of the sloop of war *Ranger* during the American War of Independence. His intention was to destroy the fleet of 200 collier vessels moored in the harbour. His commando-style raid took place at night, but due to the defection of one of his crew, who alerted the town, he was forced to retreat having accomplished very little. However, John Paul Jones's attack on Whitehaven remains the last invasion of the English mainland in over two centuries.

After the American War of Independence, having lost its tobacco and slave trade, and almost a hundred vessels to privateers, Whitehaven's once leading position among Britain's ports steadily declined. The waters of the Solway proved too shallow for the rapidly increasing size of merchant ships and trade moved to deep-water ports such as Glasgow and Liverpool. The coming of the railways, too, hastened the end of the Cumbrian ports.

By the late nineteenth century, Whitehaven was experiencing a severe recession. This continued right through the 1920s and '30s, and even the new industries which were set up before and after the Second World War did little to improve the situation. Unlike so many towns which constantly replaced old buildings, Whitehaven's town centre barely changed for a century. For this reason it now contains a remarkably high proportion its of Georgian heritage. Recent developments have been directed towards retaining these old buildings wherever possible and adapting them to present-day needs. Where demolition has proved unavoidable, redevelopment has generally been sensitively designed to blend in with the traditional buildings of the town.

In 1965 the Council for British Archaeology conducted a survey of towns worthy of preservation for their architectural merit. Within the Cumberland and Westmorland area only two towns, Whitehaven and Cockermouth, were awarded the designation 'Gem Towns' among a total of fifty-one so recognized throughout Great Britain. As Whitehaven's old buildings are gradually restored, the town is steadily emerging from generations of poverty and neglect and tourists are beginning to explore this 'forgotten port' which once dominated the maritime affairs of north-west England.

SECTION ONE

The Town and its Buildings

In 1991 the Royal Commission on the Historical Monuments of England published a monograph entitled *Whitehaven 1660–1800*. Few such volumes devoted to individual towns have been undertaken by the Royal Commission, and Whitehaven was selected because surprisingly few buildings in the central area have been demolished or radically altered during the last 200 years.

The town's period of greatest prosperity was in the mid-eighteenth century when the grid-like pattern laid down a century earlier was more or less complete. Many of the groups of larger houses had generous garden plots and the buildings were generally well designed and soundly constructed. By the end of the century the town and its harbour had begun to decline due largely to the emergence of deep-water ports capable of accommodating larger vessels.

While the international trade diminished, the demands of the Irish coal trade continued to rise. Still more manpower was required for the pits and the open spaces in the town centre were filled with rows of cheaply built terraced houses. Many of the larger properties were divided to provide accommodation for several families. The water supply and sanitation became inadequate, and by the middle of the nineteenth century the town contained many areas of slums. In 1849 a Public Health Act report on Whitehaven was compiled by Robert Rawlinson, who commented: 'The town and suburbs of Whitehaven are very unhealthy and particularly liable to epidemic and endemic diseases at all levels.' J.S. Bristowe (Medical Inspector) reported further in 1863: 'The close packing together of houses which forms one of the most serious evils . . . is not otherwise remediable than by reconstruction of a large part of the town.' Although Rawlinson's comprehensive and damning report was acted upon, no action was taken on Bristowe's comment; there was neither the will nor the necessary capital to redevelop the town for over a century. A proposed wholesale destruction of the Georgian heart of Whitehaven actually commenced in the late 1960s. Most of the properties between the harbour and Strand Street were demolished and an ugly, if functional, multi-storey car park was erected on Swingpump Lane. It was intended that this 'development' should proceed in phases but, most fortunately, in the early '70s there was a complete reappraisal of the situation. The importance of the town's architectural heritage was recognized, and instead of destruction a policy of conservation was adopted. Many of the jerry-built Victorian houses have been demolished but, with few exceptions, 'in-fill' buildings have

WHITEHAVEN, 1859. One of the earliest surviving photographs of the town, this general view was reissued as a postcard *c.* 1900. Features of interest include the large building, left foreground, which was the National School (later rebuilt as St James's Church School), Wellington Pit, overlooking the sea, top left, and the shipyards, extreme right. The impressive building with pillars near the shipyard was an hotel. It was built in 1845 as the Lonsdale Hotel, but was later leased to the Furness Junction Railway as offices. When Bransty station was completed the railway's offices were accommodated there, and the hotel reopened as the Grand Hotel. It survived until 1942 when it was destroyed by fire.

been designed to blend in with the surrounding townscape. Large numbers of buildings have been restored and new street furniture and paved areas are steadily improving the appearance and living standards in the town. There are still some unsightly blemishes, but during the next few years these should be eradicated and Whitehaven will live up to its designation as one of England's 'Gem Towns'.

ST JAMES'S CHURCH, 1859. Also reissued as a postcard, this shows St James's church which was designed by the region's most outstanding mining engineer, Carlisle Spedding, in 1752. It is described as having the finest Georgian church interior in the county. Beyond, the great arms of the piers reach out into the Solway.

WHITEHAVEN, *c.* 1905, viewed from the opposite side of town. The long row of tiny houses running diagonally from bottom right were built as miners' dwellings around 1788, and survived until demolished in the late 1940s. The large sheds behind them belonged to the Preston Street railway goods yard. It will be noted that the town nestles snugly in a valley between the hills.

VIEW OF THE SPORTS FIELD, *c.* 1950. Beyond the tall modern building of West Cumberland College, a huge stone mansion stands amongst the trees. This is Whitehaven Castle, former home of the Whitehaven branch of the Lowther family, owners of the estate. Examine the outline formed by the trees of Castle Park; it is in the shape of a rabbit or hare! This is no accident. It was deliberately planned this way, and next to it another group of trees is in the shape of an antique pistol. It is claimed that there were other such plantings, including a fish.

CHURCH STREET, 1968. The Lowthers' plan for the development of the town decreed that all buildings should be three storeys high and, to this day, there are very few exceptions to this rule. However, as there was no prescribed height for the storeys, there is a great diversity of roof levels. This prevents a boring barrack-like uniformity within the rows of houses. In the foreground is Collis pawnshop, the last in the town, surviving until the 1970s.

CHURCH STREET, 1962. A row of period houses. Shortly afterwards, one of them was demolished and replaced by a modern shop. The disastrous result can be seen below.

CHURCH STREET, 1962/63. Beuna Fashions, just after completion, sits uncomfortably between traditional buildings. It remains, thankfully, one of the few modern buildings *not* designed to blend with its surroundings. There is a place for such buildings, but the heart of a Georgian town is not that place.

CHURCH STREET, 1974. A group of old houses sympathetically restored. Character and individuality have been retained, but do not conflict with the original pattern.

ROMAN CATHOLIC CHURCH OF ST BEGH'S, COACH ROAD, *c.* 1920. Designed by Edward Welby Pugin and built 1864–8, this fine church lost much of its external character when the ornate spire was declared dangerous and had to be removed in 1931.

ST BEGH'S CHURCH INTERIOR, *c.* 1920.

CORKICKLE, *c.* 1905. A row of fine large houses. The roadway was formerly paved with wooden blocks so that miners on their way to work would cause less noise and disturbance to the occupants.

HAMILTON TERRACE, CORKICKLE, 1971. A beautifully proportioned row of fine town houses.

DUKE STREET, *c.* 1890. The impressive Victorian building on the left is an example of a style known as 'Whitehaven Italianate'. The nearer building, the 'Chusan Tea Warehouse', was subsequently rebuilt on a much grander scale which almost rivalled its neighbour.

LIFEBOAT PARADE, DUKE STREET, 1903. In 1903 a new lifeboat was delivered to Whitehaven. It was towed proudly round the streets to raise money for its upkeep. Note the two buildings (left) shown in the previous photograph; the Chusan Tea Warehouse has now been rebuilt

GRAVES BROS, PAWNBROKERS. 15 Duke Street, *c.* 1920.

NOS 13 AND 14 FOXHOUSES ROAD, 1970. Perhaps the most striking feature of the many fine houses on this road is the elegance of their stepped doorways. These two photographs give an indication of their variety and, sometimes, inconvenience!

NOS 17 AND 18 FOXHOUSES ROAD, 1970.

THE RED LION INN, Hamilton Lane, just before its demolition in 1958. The town contained many areas of neglected Victorian 'in-fill' buildings, but very few of these jerry-built properties remain. They are gradually being restored to acceptable standards or rebuilt in keeping with the basically Georgian townscape.

KING STREET, 1911. The Beehive Drapery establishment. This firm continued with very little change until the 1970s, and was still using a central cash desk linked to the sales areas by pneumatic change delivery tubes.

KING STREET, *c.* 1925. Hardly a rival to the Beehive emporium, Hull's shop specialized in corsets and underwear.

NO. 27 KING STREET, 1893. The staff at the entrance of Wilson & Kitchin's chemist shop.

KING STREET, *c.* 1910, viewed towards Duke Street from Lowther Street crossroads. This was probably taken on a market day (Thursday or Saturday).

LOWTHER STREET. The Old Public Offices, *c.* 1890. Around 1910 this building with its audacious, almost theatrical, sweep of steps was demolished and replaced by a much larger building. This now houses the town's main post office and the local studio of Radio Cumbria. Pity the steps had to go!

LOWTHER STREET METHODIST CHURCH, 1910. This church is faced with random granite, quite unlike any other building in the town.

LOWTHER STREET, ST NICHOLAS' CHURCH, 1899. The third church to occupy this site, St Nicholas' was gutted by fire on 31 August 1971. Only the tower still stands.

ST NICHOLAS' CHURCH, 1800. Taken from a pen-and-wash drawing, this shows the second church on the site, which was demolished to allow the construction of the third.

LOWTHER STREET decorated for the Coronation of Edward VII. The wet day does not appear to have dampened local enthusiasm too much.

CASTLE GROUNDS, LOWTHER STREET, 1899. Snow does not often fall in Whitehaven, and when it does it rarely 'sticks'.

LOWTHER STREET, 1899. The splendid buildings on the left all remain. The one with the arch on the right has long since disappeared, and the adjoining, darker building later housed the town's museum until it was demolished in the 1950s. The extension to the public library now occupies this site. At the far end of the road can be seen the corner of Whitehaven Castle, the home of the Lowther family.

LOWTHER STREET at the junction with King Street, *c.* 1925. The fine building facing us (Ridout & Bennets, outfitters) has been replaced, but there are few other changes

PETER LEECH'S SHOP, 26 Lowther Street. A large consignment of tea is being delivered to the shop.

MARKET PLACE, *c.* 1910. The building behind the street-lamp is the Golden Lion Hotel. Earlier, this had been the port's Customs and Excise office. The area between the horse and cart and Dalzell's shop was known as the Green Market. It was segregated from the rest of the market by cast iron bollards (locally known as 'stobbs') and was formerly used only for the sale of produce from the Lowthers' estate gardens.

MARKET PLACE, *c.* 1905. In the foreground is the green market. To the right stands a temperance refreshment room where only drinks such as cocoa and lemonade were served.

MARKET HALL, 1875. This distinctive covered market was erected in 1814 and survived until 1880 when it was demolished and replaced by the much larger building shown on p. 33.

Opposite page: BRITAIN'S CIRCUS PARADE through the Market Place, *c.* 1910. This photograph shows an elephant belonging to Britain's circus drawing a large coach through the Market Place. Few buildings can have had more varied usage, serving initially as a market produce hall with an assembly room above, but subsequently becoming in turn cinema, billiard hall, tie factory and public lavatories. During the great depression it became the dole office. Scheduled for demolition in the early 1970s, it was reprieved in 1974 and converted into the town's museum, but due to structural defects, the Museum was moved to the Civic Hall on Lowther Street from 1987. At the time of writing, the Market Hall is about to be restored and converted once more, this time to shop units with a youth centre above. The museum, currently housed in temporary accommodation at the Civic Hall, is to be relocated in a purpose-built Heritage Centre on the harbour side.

BRITAIN'S CIRCUS PARADE through the Market Place, about 1910.

LEECH'S SHOP, 58 MARKET PLACE, *c.* 1920. This furniture and upholstery store was established in 1906.

WALTER WILLSON'S GROCERS SHOP, MARKET PLACE, *c.* 1900. Although now a small supermarket, this shop is still operated by Messrs Willsons.

MARK LANE, 1958. A graphic illustration of the sort of dereliction which so marred the town until well into the third quarter of the present century. There were dozens of such areas in Whitehaven, but the majority have now been restored or replaced.

NEW HOUSES, NEWTOWN. To accommodate the army of miners needed to work their coal mines, the Lowther family built hundreds of very basic houses. These were held rent-free, but the act was not a purely charitable one, the perquisite being allowed for in wage levels. Tied houses provided a substantial degree of stability in the available work-force. New Houses, which was built in the late eighteenth century survived until the 1940s when the three huge rows were demolished. In all, there were some 266 houses on this site, while hundreds more were situated on the ill-named Mount Pleasant overlooking the harbour.

MINERS' DWELLINGS, believed to be part of the ill-named 'Mount Pleasant', overlooking the harbour.

NEW ROAD, 1899. The approach to Whitehaven from the north formerly wound its way along the cliff tops, but later New Road was constructed to give a wider and more convenient route. The wooded slopes on either side still remain.

THE SHAKESPEARE PUBLIC HOUSE, Roper Street, decorated for the coronation of George V.

ROPER STREET. Roans shop window, *c.* 1910. This firm specialized in leather goods.

SCOTCH STREET, *c.* 1900. Beyond the Methodist chapel, shown separately on p. 26, stands the Congregational church. The building on the right was demolished to provide the site for the present Civic Hall. In those days traffic was so scarce, and so noisy, that one could walk blithely along the middle of the main streets.

CONGREGATIONAL CHURCH, Scotch Street, *c*. 1900.

SCOTCH STREET TANNERY just before demolition in 1958. The distinctive elevated passage spanning Scotch Street linked two parts of the tannery buildings.

HOLY TRINITY CHURCH, Scotch Street, *c.* 1905. This fine church, erected in 1715, could accommodate a congregation of 1,200. It was demolished in 1947 and its graveyard forms an attractive garden.

CEILING IN 109 SCOTCH STREET, *c.* 1950. Many of the more opulent town houses featured splendid plasterwork, of which this was a fair example.

TANGIER STREET, BRANSTY ARCH. Busy Tangier Street posed a logistical problem for those transporting coal from the Whingill group of coal mines to the harbour. The solution was the erection of this rather splendid bridge, completed in 1804. Wagons ran along wooden trestles erected on either side of the arch, but the wooden structures had been removed long before this photograph was taken, leaving the arch a pointless but attractive architectural feature. The arch forms a backdrop for the Lady Margaret charabanc about 1925. Through the arch can be glimpsed part of the Grand Hotel and Bransty station. The arch was demolished in 1927.

TANGIER STREET, GRAND HOTEL, *c.* 1910. The curved façade of Whitehaven's largest hotel dominated the end of Tangier Street until it was destroyed by fire in 1942. To its left lies the railway station. To the right two roads are seen: the one adjacent to the hotel is the original road leading out of town via Bransty Hill; the one on the right is New Road, shown on p. 36.

THE IMPOSING SIDE OF THE HOTEL. Its name was no exaggeration, and it contained one of the finest ballrooms in northern England.

TANGIER STREET, *c.* 1925. Bransty arch can be seen and, beyond it, Bransty. The arch, built to carry coal wagons over Tangier Street to the harbour, hampered traffic, and was demolished in 1927. In 1902, when a new lifeboat was acquired, it was towed round the town, but on reaching the arch the top of its mast was smashed off to the great embarrassment of the organizers.

SUNNY HILL FESTIVAL passing the same point in Tangier Street one wet day in 1906.

NO. 19 TANGIER STREET, *c.* 1890. The ironmongers and ship chandlers shop owned by W.R. Hinde, who can be seen in the doorway. The shop, although in different ownership, is still an ironmongers.

TANGIER STREET, *c.* 1939. The recently built Cumberland Motor Services bus station is seen on the right. Bransty arch had been demolished by this time, allowing the double-decker buses access to the whole town.

NO. 35 TANGIER STREET, 1905. H.S. Jacques & Co.'s garage was in Whitehaven's *avant garde* with respect to current technology for, in addition to catering for the new-fangled horseless carriages, they installed electrical equipment and telephones.

VIEWS OF THE HARBOUR FROM TANGIER STREET, *c.* 1888. Taken a few yards apart on the same day, this photograph and the next give a flavour of the town in the late nineteenth century. The one above shows a display of posters on hoardings owned by John Leathers.

A VIEW OF THE HARBOUR from Tangier Street, *c.* 1888.

TANGIER STREET. WAVERLEY TEMPERANCE HOTEL, *c.* 1900. Built in 1685 by Captain Senhouse, this was originally called Tangier House, and the name was adopted for the street. Senhouse was one of several local merchants who made a considerable fortune trading with the New World. This building was later extensively remodelled, including the insertion of dormer windows, a feature rare in Whitehaven. It remains a hotel but no longer subscribes to the Temperance movement.

SECTION TWO

The Harbour

A small stream called Pow Beck now enters Whitehaven harbour through a culvert between the Sugar Tongue and the wall of South Beach. Although the casual passer-by would scarcely notice this trickle of water, the flow of Pow Beck over thousands of years was responsible for gouging out a channel which made possible the development of Whitehaven harbour. In the earliest stages the small fishing vessels would simply have been drawn up onto the beach above tide level, but once the Irish coal trade commenced far better facilities were required to load the larger vessels needed for this trade. First a wall was constructed along the South Beach allowing vessels to be moored alongside, but around 1634 a stone-built jetty now known as Old Quay was commenced at right angles to this wall. It was extended in 1665 and 1687, and an 'elbow' added in 1809. Meanwhile other quays were being built – Sugar Tongue between 1733 and 1735, and Lime Tongue in 1754. Further moorings were provided along South Beach, and a sea wall was built extending from the north side of the harbour. As trade continued to expand additional quays were built, culminating in the construction of North Pier (1833–41) and West Pier (1824–38). The latter was designed by the great civil engineer John Rennie (1794–1874). The final phase of harbour development was the belated construction of a wet dock known as Queens Dock between 1872 and 1876 covers 4.75 acres, too small to reverse the decline of the port. During the Second World War two Jewish refugees fled from Germany and set up a small business in London. Their premises were bombed and the pair moved to Whitehaven where they commenced making fire-lighters in a small back street. Later their tiny business grew to become an enormous chemical plant situated on a hill overlooking the town. 'Marchon' became a major local employer, producing mainly detergents. It was Marchon's need for phosphate rock, imported from Africa, that kept the harbour in business for many years. Large bulk carriers were moored offshore, the crushed rock being off-loaded onto smaller vessels which could be accommodated in Queens Dock. A huge conveyor belt then carried the phosphate to silos for transportation by road to the factory. In 1992 the firm, now part of the international Albright & Wilson company announced that it would cease importation of rock phosphate and would no longer require the use of Queens Dock. Although this is undoubtedly a serious setback to the Harbour Commissioners, the port has survived previous calamities such as the loss of the transatlantic trade, and in the 1970s the shipment of coal. The future appears to lie with the leisure industry, and to this end the surrounding area is being redeveloped to attract private boat owners to the historic port. In future, yachts may take the place of the collier brigs which once brought prosperity to the ports of West Cumbria.

IRON ORE QUAY, *c.* 1858. This is probably the oldest surviving photograph of Whitehaven. It shows the timber-built pier erected for the iron ore trade. Several trucks can be seen on the railway lines which ran to the end of the pier. Cumberland iron ore was the purest obtainable and vast quantities were exported, largely to South Wales, for almost a century. Later, the Bessemer steel-making process was greatly improved, allowing the use of cheaper, less pure ores which were imported mainly from Spain. This greatly reduced the value of Cumbrian ore, and the iron ore quay eventually became redundant.

GENERAL VIEW OF THE HARBOUR FROM BRANSTY, *c.* 1880. At the bottom right two horse-drawn vehicles stand at the entrance to the railway station. The large glass-roofed building also belonged to the railway, but the long narrow sheds behind this where two vessels are on the stocks belonged to the shipyard. Most of the piers are clearly visible.

A CLOSER VIEW OF THE SHIPYARD, about 1885, not long before its closure. Note the huge wave breaking over West Pier.

HARBOUR SEEN FROM THE GRAND HOTEL, about 1900. Three empty coal wagons, known as 'chaldrons' can be seen to the left of the railway sheds. These overlook the wet dock, completed in 1876, opened 22 November that year, and named Queens Dock. Two sailing vessels are clearly visible near to the dock gates.

THERE ARE MANY INTERESTING FEATURES on this photograph of 1969. The large silo, top left, had been recently built for storing crushed phosphate rock imported by the local detergent manufacturer Marchon, now owned by Messrs Albright & Wilson. At the foot of this stand a row of coal trucks. These would either be loaded into a waiting collier vessel or taken on the main line at Bransty to fuel the steelworks at Workington. The sloping ramp, bottom left, was fitted with rails and used during the Second World War to allow large triangular targets to be lowered into the sea at high tide. These targets would be towed, on a very long hawser, behind a ship, to be used for target practice by aeroplanes operating from the RAF airfield at Silloth to the north. There was a shipyard situated in a basin behind the curved harbour wall, centre foreground. In order to allow the railway line to operate and ships to be launched there had been a swing-bridge at this point. This is illustrated on p. 69.

A SCREW-STEAMER, A SAILING VESSEL AND A PADDLE STEAMER, are seen in this postcard of about 1904. The huge masonry slope to the right is a retaining wall belonging to the spectacular Wellington Pit. Half way up this wall runs a wagonway. Small bridges at intervals along this line carried wagons to the 'hurries', chutes through which coal was loaded on to the waiting vessel.

A GENERAL VIEW OF THE ROW OF HURRIES along West Strand, 1900. The public house on the left was the Blue Anchor Inn.

Opposite: HURRIES, *c.* 1920. A horse-drawn chaldron wagon has been drawn over the chute. A lever is used to release the hinged bottom of the wagon, allowing coal to stream down the chute into the hold of the vessel below. The horse is then led to the back of the chaldron to take it away and bring another one. A laborious process, but still quicker than hand loading.

SUGAR TONGUE, *c.* 1910. This pier was used by ships unloading sugar from the West Indies. It was entirely covered, so forming a warehouse. The trade declined rapidly from the mid-nineteenth century, and Sugar Tongue was then used mainly for 'fitting out' ships launched from the yards. A portion of the warehouse was demolished in April 1929. The remaining section was destroyed by fire in 1947, and the quay is now used by fishing vessels.

THIS VIEW OF THE WESTERN SIDE OF THE HARBOUR was taken from the 'battlements' of Wellington Pit. In the bottom left corner is the Wellington public house, in front of which stand the remains of the old fort which was captured by John Paul Jones during his raid on the harbour. The nearer of the two piers is called, somewhat confusingly, Old New Quay. The outer one, designed by the great civil engineer Sir John Rennie, is named West Pier.

WAVES BREAKING OVER WEST PIER. When a high tide is accompanied by a following wind, enormous waves sometimes rise higher than the top of the lighthouse.

THE LIGHTHOUSE ON WEST PIER about 1920. This and the North Pier lighthouse are still in constant use, marking the harbour entrance.

THE NORTH PIER LIGHTHOUSE, *c.* 1905. This is much smaller than the one on West Pier, but it is delightfully designed. Sadly, the attractive ironwork steps and balcony no longer grace the tower.

THE FIRST 'LIGHTHOUSE' AT WHITEHAVEN, erected *c.* 1700. This was a lookout point, but is believed to have been topped with a brazier which was lit at night to mark the end of the pier. The building next to it housed the West Harbour Master's office and a small mortuary, where bodies recovered from the sea were placed pending investigation and burial.

SUNDIAL MOUNTED ON THE WATCHTOWER. This bears the date 1730, but was probably added at a date later than the erection of the tower.

FISH VENDORS AND CUSTOMERS at the end of Sugar Tongue, *c.* 1890.

BEACON MILL UNDER CONSTRUCTION, 1907. This huge flour mill was completed in 1909 by John Pattinson. It was built adjacent to the wet dock, on the site of a former shipyard. Pattinson's own ships tied up at the docks and were able to load and unload directly into the mill. In 1949 it was taken over by Quaker Oats Ltd who retained it until its demolition in 1975.

WHITEHAVEN -

An Outline History

by **HARRY FANCY, A.M.A., Curator, Whitehaven Museum**

WHITEHAVEN, AN OUTLINE HISTORY

As the last Ice Age gradually drew to a close, the enormous glaciers which covered much of the British Isles receded Northwards, revealing a scarred land of gigantic lakes, torrential rivers, jagged moraines and screes, and tracts of alluvial silt. This bleak landscape was steadily transformed into open moorlands, dense forests, treacherous marshes and rich pastures which were quickly populated with herds of animals and flocks of waterfowl. Tribes of hunters followed in the wake of this abundant game, crossing over low land from the European Continent. As it melted, the enormous ice-sheet caused the sea-level to rise, thus forming the English Channel, and giving the British Isles their present outline.

Described in one brief paragraph, one might imagine that this migration was rather akin to the Biblical story of the Children of Israel passing through the waters of the Red Sea, which closed behind them to cut off the pursuing Egyptians! In fact, the land bridge probably existed for centuries, during which whole tribes might migrate with seasons, until eventually the deepening channel became a serious obstacle.

During the period of the Stone Age Hunters, the Lake District appears to have been but sparsely populated, although there was an "Axe factory" at Langdale, where the stone was found to be very suitable for making tools. It seems likely that these primitive craftsmen would have worked for a few weeks or possibly months at a time, forming "rough-outs". These would be taken elsewhere for finishing, by careful re-touching and polishing to produce a fine cutting edge. The completed, or possibly the partially formed implements were exported to many parts of the country, suggesting either periodic tribal migrations or, more likely, a definite trading activity. Modern methods of petrological examination have proved that implements found hundreds of miles away were made from stone originally from this area. This view is supported by the large number of "wasters" which are still to be found in Langdale; these indicate the fabrication of enormous numbers of implements, far more than would have been required for purely local use. Actual **settlements** of the Neolithic period are very uncommon, although one fine example was discovered during draining operations at Ehenside Tarn in 1869—71. A Mesolithic settlement at Eskmeals was recently excavated by the British Museum, where many finds from this area are housed.

Significant finds from the Bronze and Iron Ages are very rare, and it has been suggested that adverse climatic conditions may have inhibited further settlement in the area during that period. It is hoped that future archaeological investigations will throw more light on the 500 years "gap" before the arrival of the Romans.

April 2nd 1987.

Walking through town's history

Mr William Reay visited Whitehaven Rambling Club recently and gave an interesting talk on the history of Whitehaven starting in the year 670, the earliest date records could be found.

The Danes and Vikings attacked the area and settled here until 945. In 1092, William Rufus captured the area and built Carlisle castle.

A priory was started in St. Bees about that period, and a dwelling was built on Prospect and St. Bees. The cliffs north of St. Bees provided good shelter for boats. Part of these cliffs were white and it became known as the haven near the white head, and was later called Whitehaven.

A small quantity of coal was found and put to good uses, small drifts were sunk on Meadow Road and Pottery Road, and the first mine shaft was at Seldom Seen.

The town grew gradually on the sea side of Pow Beck. There was deep sand here at the time and special foundations had to be built for the houses in the centre of the town.

In 1250, the first big mansion was built called the flat by the Lowther family, later to be called The Castle.

LOWTHERS

In the 17th Century the Priory sold much of its land to the Lowthers and Christopher Lowther build the first pier which attracted much shipping and coal was exported to Ireland. In time, new industries were set up and houses were build over the beautiful gardens on Mount Pleasant and eventually became slums.

John Lowther developed the land west of Scotch Street. Many newcomers were attracated to the town, and because of housing shortages many residents in the town had to live over their shops.

In 1894, the town became a Borough and James Lowther built 270 houses around Ginns.

PUMPED

Ship building was started by the Lowthers and it was a great success, bringing many new people and industries into the town, which became the second largest seaport in England.

The coming of the railways competed with shipping and the town lost most of its American trade, and the shipbuilding was moved to Liverpool.

Water was a problem in those days, and much of its drinking water was supplied by sinking wels and in 1761 water was pumped from near Stanley Pond and people had to pump their drinking water from pumps set up around the town, 11 in all.

In 1852, water was first pumped from Ennerdale, and this was greatly increased in 1947. In 1850, the sewerage system was introduced.

Over 5,000 houses have been built by the Borough Cuncil since 1920. Saltom was the first deep coal mine.

Gas street lighting was introduced in 1830 and this was succeeded in 1893 by Electric street lamps, Whitehaven was one of the first town in England to be lit by electricity.

Mr Reay mentioned many of the main industries which used to exist in the area but most of them were now extinct. Some of those used to employ a about 200 workers. Mr Reay was thanked by Norman Jackson, who presided.

Hartsop Magic is favourite to retain the HTA senior title, but note the warning sounded by the 1985 joint champion, Tudor Prince, in winning his final trials at Dean Cross and Calebreak in the space of three days.

Prince sounds

Alan Weir has high hopes of hanging on to the championship trophy which Hartsop Magic won with a total of 26 last season. But he expects a much tougher contest, with Magic up against some of last season's leading puppies in the Keswick and Westmorland fell trails.

Hartsop Magic has been broken down for 12 weeks and Alan does not expect her to strike consistent form until May. "I will be disappointed if she doesn't ticket, but don't expect her to win for a while yet," he told me on Tuesday.

So the pretenders to the crown can enhance their chances with an early run of success.

Tudor Prince and Jennings Lad fought out a close finish to the Dean Cross trials on Saturday. There were 97 hounds entered, but at Calebreak on Monday 104 seniors were slipped. Again Tudor Prince was ever prominent and drew clear of Gill Breeze and Mikado on the finish.

Mal Reay's Frizington puppy, Zulu, won at Millom on Saturday and Monday to complete a treble in the trials series there.

Warlord beat Rydal Lass and Beulah on Saturday at Millom, but on Monday Warlord was five lengths second to Rosalita.

Bill Meagan's Cleator Moor puppy, Crowgarth, has shown good early form. After beating Geordie Lass

hound owners enter into the spirit of things both could produce some interesting inter-area rivalry.

A challenge trophy and prizemoney of £100 (more if sponsorship permits) will go to the area gaining most points in a league competition being organised by HTA vice-chairman Roy Laidler.

Roy believes the league contest will not only add to the weekly interest, but will encourage hound owners to travel more into other's areas and create competition on a collective basis.

The league programme covers 63 fixtures from May to October. Each of the seven areas will be involved in 18 matches (six home, six away and six on neutral ground) and will

Caesar and his followers "Came, saw and conquered" much of Britain, establishing law and order, a network of splendid roads, important cities and hosts of forts and villas. There were sporadic outbursts of rebellion, but gradually Roman rule was imposed upon the majority of the native British tribes. Hadrian commenced his magnificent wall to protect the Northern boundary of the Empire around 120 A.D. This stupendous piece of military engineering, over 73 miles long, was completed in less than 20 years. Despite deliberate destruction and centuries of robbing of its stone for building purposes, it still stands over six feet high in places.

The remains of numerous Roman forts and settlements survive in Cumbria, Carlisle, Hardknott, Ravenglass, Maryport, Moresby and many other sites having been excavated by archaeologists and antiquarians over a period of several hundred years. Finds from such places are to be seen in various museums in the region, and the remains still standing at Hardknott are well worth visiting.

Following the departure of the Romans (407—411 A.D.) Cumbria was pillaged and sometimes settled by successive waves on invaders — Angles, Danes, Vikings, English, Scots and finally the Normans, who captured Carlisle in 1092 and began to restore order. Several castles were built (e.g. Egremont, Cockermouth and Millom) and about 1125 the Priory of St. Bees was established on the site of a former Anglian Church. This originally accommodated a prior and six monks. Subsequent gifts of land, churches, tithes and various rights, such as saltmaking, fishing and the gathering of firewood, stone and coal, led to a sustained build-up of the wealth and power of the Priory. By the mid 14th century its lands covered the whole of the present parish of St. Bees, with isolated areas of land elsewhere. At that time, Whitehaven was regarded merely as its port and was virtually uninhabited.

Two years after the first of two Acts bringing about the Dissolution of the Monasteries (1536 and 1539) by Henry VIIIth, the Priory was abolished. Certain of its properties were disposed of by the King, but the Manor, with its various rights, were retained by the Crown until 1553, when Edward VIth granted them to Thomas Chaloner. In 1559 Thomas (by then **Sir** Thomas) Chaloner sold the Manor of St. Bees to Thomas Wybergh, who mortgaged it in the following year to one George Lowther.

With the closure of the Priory and the acquisition of the Manor by the Lowther family, there was a dramatic change in the relative importance of St. Bees and Whitehaven. This change was brought about by a combination of circumstances which resulted in the emergence of Whitehaven as a major sea port. In order to understand the subsequent development of the whole area, it is essential to consider several inter-related factors — local resources, topographical problems, technological innovations and, perhaps above all, the vision, ambition and ingenuity of several local personalities.

George Lowther's newly acquired estate was situated on a considerable coal-field, but, hemmed in by mountains, the transportation of coal in bulk to other regions was economically impossible **excepting by sea.** The very name White**haven** indicates the early recognition of the natural advantages of the bay to shipping, but exportation of coal by sea would clearly entail the construction of proper harbour facilities. Ships were needed. At first these were brought from other ports, but it would be a great advantage if ships could be built and repaired locally.

Large-scale developments of this type could only take place if the necessary man-power were available, and as already indicated, the town of Whitehaven barely existed as such at that time. Skilled shipwrights, carpenters and chandlers would be required, seamen to man the ships they built, and most essential of all, labour to mine the coal and load the vessels in the harbour. This influx of workers would have to be fed and housed. A programme of building would have to be commenced, and this would require architects, quarrymen, brick-makers and builders. The needs of this rapidly growing community necessitated further growth; shops, churches, public houses, improved roads, water supplies, etc., promoted further growth and bringing still more newcomers to the area. These newcomers would also have to be housed and fed . . . There could be no half measures; if coal was to be exploited on a large scale, a rapid build-up of population was inevitable.

It is known from a survey in 1566 that Whitehaven, which at that time consisted of six fishermen's cottages*, possessed a single boat, the "Bee" of about nine tons. Sixteen years later, there were but twelve small ships in the whole of Cumberland. By 1685, when the coal trade with Ireland was still in its infancy, Whitehaven already had some 46 vessels, averaging about 43 tons, and in 1755, when the trade was firmly established, 260 vessels averaging about 115 tons were operating from this port. A substantial proportion of these ships would have been built in the town's own shipyards.

This dramatic cycle of development was initiated four years after Christopher Lowther took over the estate in 1630, for it was in 1634 that he constructed a pier to facilitate the exportation of coal to Dublin. It was, however, his heir, John, who was mainly responsible for the spectacular development of Whitehaven during the second half of the 17th Century.

* This reference to "six fishermen's cottages" could well be misleading. The survey was concerned solely with the harbour area and would not have taken into account dwellings situated further inland. Even so, we can be certain that the population would have been very sparse indeed at that time.

John, later **Sir** John Lowther, was born in 1642, when the population of the town is estimated to have been about 250. By the time of his death in 1705, it housed over 2,000. The town was planned with great care on a "grid-iron" pattern which is still clearly visible despite much subsequent "in-fill" building. It was this later development which was to result in serious overcrowding, bad sanitation, disease and general squalor during the 19th and 20th Centuries; the original plan had been abandoned in favour of high density housing. To some extent greed had replaced vision.

The coal trade with Dublin flourished, and tobacco, sugar, and other commodities were later imported on a considerable scale from the New World. In Sir John's time, Whitehaven's merchant fleet of 77 vessels was amongst the largest in Britain; his mines were very productive, the harbour greatly improved and a limited amount of ship-building was being undertaken.

In 1705 Sir John's second son James inherited the estate (and at a later date, the title) and took over the responsibility for the further development of the town until his death at the age of 81 in 1755.

Meanwhile two major technological developments had occurred — the invention of the steam engine, and the discovery that iron could be smelted and worked by means of coal rather than the costly charcoal used until that time. These innovations were to have far-reaching effects upon the future progress of the whole region.

The earliest steam engines, more correctly known as "atmospheric engines", were terribly inefficient, operating as they did at very low pressure. These ponderous machines, never-the-less were the "prime movers" of the Industrial Revolution.

The depth to which a coal mine can be worked depends upon many factors, the most crucial of which is often the efficiency of the pumps used to drain the workings. For centuries simple engines powered by horses were used for this purpose, and for winching coal up and down the shaft, but there was clearly a limit to the power of such "horse ginns". The steam engine opened up tremendous possibilities by allowing even deeper seams to be drained and worked. Although shallow pits were sunk in this area during the 16th Century, and surface and sea-shore gathering of coal would have been practised long before this, the first attempts to exploit coal commercially for export rather than merely to supply local needs, appear to have commenced around 1620. By 1663 several shafts had been sunk, in which drainage was achieved by means of special underground passages and by the use of horse ginns, but the first atmospheric engine in the area was installed around 1715 in that part of Whitehaven which is still known as "The Ginns". Although horse ginns continued to be used at many local mines for a considerable length of time after this date, the steam engine soon proved its worth, and became indispensible when deeper workings were driven.

The first really powerful engine was installed in 1780, and by 1843 two shafts had been sunk to 840 feet, a depth quite beyond the limitations of horse ginns. Surprisingly, however, steam engines were initially used only for pumping, but it was later realised that they could also be used for winding, that is hauling men, materials and coal up and down the shaft. Wicker baskets called Corves were used as containers for the coal, and in the days of the horse ginn these held only about 2½ cwt. Steam winding permitted the use of corves holding 12 cwt., which greatly speeded up the extraction of coal. Such corves were, remarkably enough, still in use at William Pit until 1875.

As in the case of ship-building, it would be a great advantage if mining equipment and steam engines could be produced locally. Fortunately several foundries already existed in the area, including a large concern at Lowca, which was to survive under various names until 1927. During its long existence, this firm built amongst other things the first iron ship in Cumberland, the 121 ton "Lowca" of 1843. A number of railway locomotives constructed at Lowca are still operating at certain steam railway preservation centres.

The foundry commenced in the 18th Century, and during the American War of Independence, when almost a hundred Whitehaven ships were sunk or captured, this firm supplied many of the cannon used for arming local ships. The need to replace those vessels lost during the war gave a considerable impetus to shipbuilding in the region, and the engineering company at Lowca profited greatly from the increased market for ships fittings. Adam Heslop designed and constructed the first rotatory winding engine in the region at this same foundry in 1791. Another engine which he built about four years later worked at Wreay and other local pits until 1878, after which it was acquired by the Science Museum, London, where it is still featured as one of the nation's major technological exhibits.

Apart from sound engineering expertise, skilled workers, premises and equipment, such an enterprise obviously required fuel, readily obtainable from local pits, and a source of iron. Fortunately, in addition to its extensive coalfield, Cumbria was rich in iron-ore. This had been exploited for centuries by means of relatively small forges and bloomeries fired with charcoal, but a new technology came into being after 1740 when Abraham Derby, of Shropshire, perfected the technique of smelting and working iron by means of coal. His discoveries, together with the later development of the blast furnace, formed another vital factor in the Industrial Revolution, allowing a tremendous expansion in the iron and steel trade. Important iron mines were developed, notably at Millom, Cleator and Beckermet, whilst smelting and processing was carried out at such places as Barrow and Workington. There is a vestige of this important industry to this day; Beckermet iron mine, the last haematite mine still worked commercially in Britain, supplies some of the ore used by the British Steel plant at Workington, and this is fired with coal from Haig Pit, the last working coal mine in Whitehaven.

The evolution of the town and port of Whitehaven, then, depended upon a number of inter-related factors: the physical geography of the region, the presence of coal and iron-ore deposits, the need for shipping and suitable harbour facilities. The pattern of development was a logical progression which continued without serious interruption from the 17th to the late 19th century.

Unfortunately for Whitehaven, and for several other ports of the Solway, this pattern began to change radically from the middle of the Victorian era, and by the end of the century, serious problems were beginning to emerge. Many of the pits which had been exploited so intensively became worked out or were closed following disasters; the port, which was tidal, could not accommodate the larger vessels being built elsewhere, and which were more economical to operate*; railways were able to break the maritime monopoly of trade in this isolated region, and allowed much more rapid communication. Finally, ship-building became progressively less viable in view of the rapidly declining coal trade and the emergence of large ships which were beyond the capacity of the small shipyards of the Solway. The last Whitehaven shipyard closed in 1889 and the last Workington-built ship was launched in 1938.

Unemployment was already a serious problem in the region before the great depression of the 1920's and 30's. Whitehaven, once one of the greatest ports in the country, and one of the North's largest and most prosperous towns, was seriously affected. As more and more pits closed and the dole queues lengthened, the town's splendid Georgian and Victorian buildings started to decay and many areas of the town degenerated into slums.

Since the Second World War new industries have been established in the district and the long decline has now been arrested. An enlightening policy of conservation of the town's rich architectural heritage has led not only to a better standard of living and a renewed sense of pride amongst the 26,000 inhabitants, but has also begun to attract a significant number of tourists and holiday makers to the area.

This mixed economy of various industries, farming, fishing and tourism offers a much sounder future than the previous structure which, in the final analysis, rested far too heavily on a single commodity which had been regarded as inexhaustible; that commodity was coal.

* The opening of the "Queen's Dock" in 1876 was too late to arrest the decline of the port, which had been completely eclipsed by developments elsewhere, particularly at Liverpool. The wet dock at Whitehaven covers about 4¾ acres and can accommodate vessels of up to 270 feet in length by 40 feet wide, with a draught of 18 feet. This asset has proved invaluable in providing docking facilities for cargo vessels engaged in the modern chemical industry.

Tourist Information Centres in Copeland
Opening Times

Whitehaven
Market Place, Whitehaven — Tel. No. Whitehaven 5678

May—Sept.	Mon.—Sat.	10 a.m.—6 p.m.
Oct.—Apr.	Mon.—Sat.	10 a.m.—4-30 p.m.

Ravenglass
Ratty Car Park, Ravenglass — Tel. Ravenglass 278

May—Sept.	Every Day	11 a.m. — 6 p.m.

Millom
St. George's Road, Millom — Tel. Millom 2555

Whit—Sept.	Mon.—Sat.	10 a.m.—5 p.m.
	Sun	1-30—5 p.m.

Egremont
Lowes Court, Main Street, Egremont — Tel. Egremont 693

May—Sept.	Mon.—Sat.	10—1 & 2—5
	Closed Wed. afternoons	

Published by the Whitehaven Tourist Information Centre, 1978
Reprinted 1980.

DOBSON & MUSGRAVE'S WAREHOUSE, West Strand, *c.* 1895. This building, now converted into flats, was the warehouse of a large provision merchant. It is adjacent to the harbour, as a great deal of its goods were brought in by sea.

MOUNT STEPS AND MAGARRY'S HOUSES, *c.* 1906. These steps still survive, although now resurfaced in concrete. They gave access to hundreds of miner's dwellings in the inappropriately named Mount Pleasant area, overlooking the south harbour. To the left of the steps can be seen the wall of the town's sewage pumping station, which from 1893 also housed the electricity generating station.

THE SHIPYARD SWING-BRIDGE, *c.* 1913. One of the shipyards was situated in a basin linked to the harbour by a narrow channel. When a railway line was laid round the harbour to the mainline at Bransty station, some way had to be found to get vessels in and out of the yard! This swing-bridge was the solution. Beyond the bridge can be seen the end of the covered Sugar Tongue, and above that some of the miners' houses of Mount Pleasant.

EAST STRAND, *c.* 1900. The notice on the wall reads 'Whitehaven Cab and General Posting Company Limited. Carters, Contractors and Furniture Removers by Road or Rail.' Later, the property became Howson's motor-cycle shop.

THE CROWD ASSEMBLED ON THE PIER is witnessing the inauguration of a new mail service to the Isle of Man in 1912. The vessel was the *Tynwald*. Pattinson's mill dominates the skyline, and to its left Bransty station is visible. The main shipyards, defunct for nearly a quarter of a century, had occupied the foreshore in front of the station.

THE OLD HARBOUR OFFICE, 1899. This delightful office, erected at the time of the construction of the wet dock in 1876, has long since disappeared. The little 0–4–0 tank locomotive, one of many used around the docks, was called the *Phoenix*.

CUSTOMS HOUSE, *c.* 1900. This fine building, erected in 1811, bears a notice over the door which reads 'Inland Revenue Customs House.' It is adjacent to Dobson & Musgrave's warehouse (see page 67) and is now owned by the charity Age Concern.

SECTION THREE

Ships and Shipbuilding

Ongoing research has identified over 1,000 vessels built in Whitehaven's shipyards. The majority of these were mundane collier vessels of 150 to 250 tons, but, later, much larger barques and ships approaching 3,000 tons were built. The first shipbuilder whose name is known was Thomas Sibson (1686–1775). How many vessels he constructed is not known. William Palmer (1702–78) built about ten vessels between 1757 and 1778. Several other eighteenth-century builders, Benjamin Hadwen, Roger Martindale and John and William Wood, are also very shadowy figures, although John Wood also established a shipyard at Workington and his brother set up a long-lived yard at Maryport. The most interesting firm was that established by Daniel Brocklebank (1725–1804). Trained as a shipwright at Whitehaven, he emigrated to Maine in America in 1770 to establish his own shipyard, taking with him his wife and a number of fellow workers. Five years later, with the American War of Independence looming, he refused to throw in his lot with the colonists, and returned to Whitehaven in his last ship, the *Castor* which was still fitting out at the time of his stealthy departure. Not being properly provisioned, they sailed first to Newfoundland where they caught a quantity of fish to feed themselves on the transatlantic voyage. Arriving safely back at Whitehaven, Captain Brocklebank proceeded to refit the *Castor* and obtained a 'Letter of Marque' allowing him to act as a privateer against American vessels. After the end of the war, Brocklebank returned to shipbuilding, constructing some twenty-seven vessels before his death. His two sons, Thomas and John, continued to run this company, until its closure in 1865, during which time they had built some 131 ships. They had also established a considerable shipping line which operated out of Liverpool and was later to merge with the Cunard line. Many other shipbuilders operated yards in Whitehaven, notably Whiteside and Scott, William Walker & Co., Lumley Kennedy & Co., and Shepherd and Leech. In 1869 a new company, the Whitehaven Shipbuilding Company, was established and built forty-two vessels, including Whitehaven's first iron-built ship *Patterdale* in 1871. Shortage of capital led to the temporary closure of the yard in 1879 but in the following year the concern was re-established as the Whitehaven Shipbuilding Company No. 2. Before the closure of this, the last yard in 1889, a further thirty-four vessels had been launched. Completion of the 2,374 ton four-masted barque Englehorn marked the end of shipbuilding at Whitehaven.

TENASSERIM UNDER CONSTRUCTION, 1861. This was the 161st vessel built by the firm of T. & J. Brocklebank, which later merged with the firm of Samuel Cunard of Liverpool. The 1,002 ton *Tenasserim* was launched on 10 August 1861, and was wrecked at Arklow in 1865. She was 195 ft long with a beam of 35 ft and draught of 22 ft.

THE SHIPYARD OF SHEPHERD & LEACH, *c.* 1871. This is believed to be the 223 ton brigantine *Beckermet*, the last vessel built by this company. She measured 107.1 ft by 23.1 ft by 35 ft, and had a draught of 22 ft.

LAUNCH OF THE *PATTERDALE*, 3 June 1871. This 1,187 ton vessel marked the beginning of the last chapter for Whitehaven shipyards. She was the first vessel built by the newly founded WSC, and the first iron ship launched at Whitehaven. This engraving appeared in the *Graphic* magazine on 8 July 1871.

WHITEHAVEN SHIPYARDS, North Shore, *c.* 1881. The small forest of vertical timbers are the 'stocks' of the shipyard, standing empty at the time of the photograph. Lines of railway wagons and coaches stand outside Bransty station.

THIRLMERE FITTING OUT ALONGSIDE SUGAR TONGUE, 1874. This 1,711 ton vessel was launched from North Shore, then towed into the harbour by steam tug to undergo completion prior to her maiden voyage.

RIGGERS POSE FOR A PHOTOGRAPH during their work aboard the *Thirlmere*. This splendid photograph illustrates the amazing complexity of the rigging of an ocean-going ship. The expression 'getting to know the ropes' is used glibly in everyday speech, but an apprentice seaman had to learn the function of every one of these ropes – the fate of the ship could hang on this knowledge.

THIRLMERE ALMOST READY FOR DEPARTURE. She is still tied up at Sugar Tongue. Note that she was registered in Liverpool; many ships were built at Whitehaven for companies in Liverpool.

THIRLMERE, the vessel furthest from the camera, about to sail. Her anchor is raised, and a tug will shortly tow her from the harbour into the open sea where her sails will be unfurled for the first time.

CAPTAIN'S RECEPTION ABOARD THE *THIRLMERE*. Note the ladies, dressed in the latest fashion; they would be the wives of owners, builders and ship's officers, invited aboard for celebrations before the ship's departure.

THE BARQUE *ALICE A. LEIGH* BEING LAUNCHED, October 1889. At 2,929 tons, this was the largest vessel ever built at Whitehaven, and she cost £25,943. Both she and her successor *Englehorn* became stuck on the ways during launching and had to be towed off by steam tugs. These were not the first vessels to experience this embarrassment – the Solway was just too shallow for building large vessels.

THE *BOYNE* OF WHITEHAVEN. This watercolour painting in Whitehaven Museum shows a typical brig as built at Whitehaven for perhaps 150 years. Dated 1794, it is one of only two known paintings by William Jackson.

OIL PAINTING OF *TRELAWNEY* BY ROBERT SALMON, 1808. Salmon, now recognized as one of the finest British marine artists, was born in Whitehaven. His father was a Jewish jeweller called Salomon, and it was probably from him that Robert inherited his meticulous eye for detail. The Whitehaven-built *Trelawney* is seen here against a backdrop of the busy harbour. The painting is in Whitehaven Museum.

MARIA LOWTHER, *c.* 1875. Built at Guernsey in 1840, this 1,070 ton schooner is seen in Whitehaven harbour. She was lost off Ireland in 1878 but her tiny figurehead is preserved in Whitehaven Museum.

CUSTOM HOUSE DOCK, 1859. The two vessels in the foreground are, left, the *Bee*, built at Harrington in 1830, and, right, the *Favourite* of Whitehaven. This very early photograph illustrates how busy the harbour was at that period.

DUNBOYNE UNDER CONSTRUCTION. The real point of interest in this photograph of 1888 is not the unidentified vessels in the foreground, but the prow of the vessel jutting up on the left. This is the only known photograph of the *Dunboyne* before her launch. Her name was subsequently changed to *G. D. Kennedy* and later to *af Chapman*. It is under the last name that she is preserved in Stockholm harbour.

af CHAPMAN, *c.* 1937. This picture was not taken at Whitehaven, for by this time she was operating as a sail-training ship for the Swedish navy.

VESSELS IN WHITEHAVEN HARBOUR, *c.* 1900. Behind them can be seen the railway sheds, Grand Hotel and, beyond, the houses of Bransty.

FISHING VESSELS in the harbour, *c.* 1890.

FOUR-MASTED BARQUE *GOLDEN GATE*, *c.* 1925. Launched as *Lord Shaftsbury* at Whitehaven in 1888, this vessel of 2,332 tons measured 293 ft by 42 ft and was a fine example of local shipbuilding craftsmanship.

ELEANOR DIXON at Whitehaven, *c.* 1860. Note the candlestick chimney on South Beach, top right. This small Irish collier vessel, for some reason now forgotten, held a captain's reception while in port. Perhaps the captain got married here, or the ship may have come under new ownership; whatever the reason, the occasion was recorded in the following splendid photographs.

RECEPTION aboard the *Eleanor Dixon*, *c*. 1860.

RECEPTION aboard the *Eleanor Dixon, c.* 1860.

Hundreds of humble collier vessels, brigs, or, a variant, the snow, were built at Whitehaven. Although small they were of extremely strong construction: built like a tiny battleship was the comment of an American archaeologist who studied the remains of the *Betsy*, sunk off Yorktown, Virginia in 1781. This strength enabled them to withstand the punishment of Atlantic gales on their voyages to the New World. However, more glamorous vessels were also built: armed merchant men, fast-sailing cargo ships for the Indian and China trades, and a small number of steamships. Of over 1,000 vessels built, only one has been properly preserved: now called the *af Chapman*, she is a tourist attraction in Stockholm harbour. Whitehaven's first paddle-steamer, the *Countess of Lonsdale*, with engines built in Liverpool, was launched here in 1827.

BUCKET DREDGER *FLEETWOOD*, 1904. Whitehaven harbour has to be constantly dredged to prevent the build-up of silt.

DREDGER *CLEARWAY* photographed in 1928, the year in which she was acquired by the Whitehaven Harbour Commissioners. Although her crane is now diesel-powered, her motive power is still steam, and she is possibly the oldest steam-driven dredger in constant use in the world today. She has been in service for some sixty-four years at the time of writing, and looks good for many years to come.

DAY EXCURSIONS TO THE ISLE OF MAN were extremely popular in the era of the paddle-steamer. Here well-dressed trippers are embarking on *Mona's Isle* at Whitehaven in 1913.

THE VERY ELEGANT PADDLE-STEAMER *PRINCESS ALICE* at the steamboat station on Sugar Tongue about 1895.

PADDLE TUG *PRINCE OF WALES* alongside Sugar Tongue, 1905.

STEAM SHIP *BUSK*, seen here around 1910, was one of the vessels owned by Beacon Mills.

SS *SAPPHIRE* LOADING IRON ORE IN QUEENS DOCK, 1895. The 384 ton steamer was built by J. Fullerton of Paisley in 1881. The chutes down which the ore was loaded into the hold are clearly visible.

MARCHON ENTERPRISE UNLOADING PHOSPHATE ROCK IN QUEENS DOCK, 1962, shortly after being commissioned. In recent years the harbour has been financed largely by the chemical industry. Founded as Marchon Chemicals during the Second World War, the firm is now part of the international firm of Albright & Wilson. *Marchon Enterprise* was the first vessel acquired by the original company.

WHITEHAVEN LIFEBOAT, *c.* 1902, Coxswain Craddock (centre) with brothers Richard (left) and Jack Wignal. All are wearing the cork life jackets of the period. In 1954 the port of Whitehaven received a vellum testimonial tribute from the Royal National Lifeboat Institution in recognition of the port's long tradition of rescue at sea. This rare honour records that Whitehaven had a lifeboat, manned by volunteers, from 1804, some years before the establishment of the RNLI. In addition to its lifeboat, the port also provided a rocket brigade which operated from the shore. When a vessel was stranded close to the shore, rockets carrying lines were fired by the brigade. Once a line was received aboard the ship, a much heavier cable was drawn across allowing a breeches-buoy rescue apparatus to be set up. Many swift rescues were effected in this way, and the coastal railway was used to convey the rocket tender to the scene of a wreck. Whitehaven's last lifeboat was taken out of service in 1925.

A PRACTICE LAUNCH, *c.* 1910.

THE LAST WHITEHAVEN LIFEBOAT, *Elizabeth Leicester II,* at the time she was withdrawn and the station closed, in 1925.

JOHN HAMPSON OF WHITEHAVEN, 1866–1923. According to his obituary, he and his father saved more than 100 people from drowning. He worked as a seaman until about 1896, then became a miner at Wellington Pit. During the disaster of 1910 (see pp. 101–3) he was on the rescue team and was one of many to receive the Edward Medal for this service.

ROCKET BRIGADE TENDER, housed on Old Quay, *c.* 1900.

ON PARADE, 20 September 1895. The tender, drawn by six horses, poses in front of the Royal Standard public house on the harbour front. The lead horse is ridden by Tom Woodend, a soldier, while Sal Madge, a well-known local personality, stands beside the last horse.

A LIFEBOAT GOING TO THE ASSISTANCE of a vessel foundering off Whitehaven. This is believed to be the *Ellen & Mary*, lost in October 1921. The lifeboat would have been *Elizabeth Leicester II*, in action four years before the Whitehaven lifeboat station was closed.

WRECK OF THE BARQUE *BENGAL*. This Norwegian vessel was driven ashore at Redness Point near Whitehaven on 15 October 1902. She became a total wreck and was sold for £61 plus £30 for her anchor cable. All the crew were saved by the Whitehaven Rocket Brigade, and King Oscar of Norway awarded medals to Captain Robert Wilson and Lieutenant Malcolm McGill, with a sum of money to be divided among their men.

THE FINNISH STEAMER *ESBO* was driven ashore at Drigg, Cumberland, in the teeth of a gale gusting up to 130 m.p.h. on 19 October 1935. A few members of the crew got to land on a ship's boat, but the remainder were rescued by breeches-buoy manned by members of the Bootle and the Whitehaven Rocket Brigades. Lifeboats from Maryport and Barrow were also called out but, due to the appalling conditions, arrived too late to be of assistance.

SS *IZARO* ASHORE ON TOMLIN ROCKS, St Bees, 25 May 1907. Strangely enough, this incident was not reported in the local press, and is still something of a mystery. The remains of her boiler can sometimes be seen at very low tide.

SECTION FOUR

Coal Mining

On a national scale, the Cumbrian coalfield is fairly small, covering only about 100 square miles, including sizeable areas beneath the Solway sea. The main or Prior Band is very substantial, reaching some 13 ft in thickness in some places. This and other bands were workable, and the coal is of good quality. Coal outcrops on the surface and is often washed up on the shore, particularly after storms. Surface pickings, shallow pits and simple adits driven into the hillside sufficed for local needs, but from the early seventeenth century, when the Lowther family started to exploit the deposits commercially, mining rapidly increased in both scale and complexity.

Unfortunately, the Cumbrian measures contained a very high measure of fire damp, the highly inflammable, often explosive gas, which is also known as methane or marsh gas. For this reason, many features of safety in colliery workings were pioneered in Whitehaven. These included the first attempt to produce a safe working light, the Spedding wheel or steel mill, invented around 1730 following the first scientific investigation of the nature of fire damp and the discovery that barometric readings could be used to warn of particularly dangerous conditions. The method of mine ventilation known as 'coursing the air' was also pioneered in Whitehaven pits, where the first form of gas mask, known as the Roberts Smoke Hood, was devised.

In addition, Whitehaven coal staiths included a huge structure known as 'the Hurries', which greatly increased the speed with which collier vessels could be loaded, and some of the first tramways for overland haulage of coal were also established to link various pits to the harbour. The Lowthers also installed some of the first atmospheric engines for colliery pumping and winding, and worked the first major under-sea mine. Despite these splendid innovations, the mines remained extremely dangerous and it is known that over 1,000 lives have been lost underground in the town and its immediate vicinity. Apart from one small adit ('walk-in') mine at St Bees, the Cumbrian coalfield is exploited only by opencast workings. The last shaft mine, Haig Pit, closed in 1986.

THIS PIT ENGINE was built at Lowca near Whitehaven around 1795. It was used for over a century, and is shown working at Low Wreah pit around 1880. A few years later it was removed to the Patent Office Museum, London, and later to the Science Museum. It was designed by Adam Heslop and was a 'rotative engine', that is, the end of the reciprocating beam turned a large fly-wheel by means of a crank. James Watt and Heslop both claimed priority for this important invention, which greatly increased the range of applications for steam power. Heslop's claim was upheld and Watt was compelled to devise the much more complicated 'sun and planet' motion to achieve the same end.

THREE 'CORVES', large baskets used to haul coal from the pit, photographed in around 1870. One is shown emerging from the shaft, and to the left, a corf has been placed on a bogie for transport by rail. The photograph was taken at William Pit not long before corves were replaced by the familiar metal 'tubs' with their own wheels.

WORKERS ON THEIR WAY TO WILLIAM PIT, *c.* 1890. Note the water bottles hanging from their shoulders. Food, known locally as 'bait', was carried in rat-proof tins. On the left is the gas works, built on the site of the shipyard.

WILLIAM PIT in 1911. A busy scene at the pit top. A group of 'screen lasses' who picked rock and shale from the coal, can be seen at the entrance to the screen shed.

WILLIAM PIT BUILDINGS, 1967, shortly before demolition. The sinking of this pit commenced in 1804. During its long existence literally dozens of explosions occurred, culminating in the second worst disaster in the Cumbrian coalfield when 114 men were killed; even before this it had been dubbed 'The most dangerous pit in the Kingdom'.

WELLINGTON PIT, *c.* 1900. Towering above the harbour, this was by far the most spectacular of Whitehaven's pits, built in the form of a castle with a great keep, turrets and enormous crenellated walls. Its twin shafts were sunk between 1840 and 1845.

DEMOLITION OF THE WELLINGTON PIT BUILDINGS, 1969. The very distinctive chimney was modelled on a candlestick owned by the Lowthers, and at one time it sported a 6 ft high metal 'flame' to stress the point. Fortunately the chimney, actually a ventilation shaft, has been retained and now serves as an escape vent for methane gas which still escapes from the old workings. The massive masonry walls, remain a splendid feature of the South Beach.

DURING THE 1910 DISASTER a local photographer compiled a graphic record of the scenes above ground. This, and the following three photographs are selected from this sequence. A group of rescue workers await their turn to descend.

A RESCUE TEAM POSES FOR THE CAMERA. The helmets, which are very similar to those worn by divers, belong to the 'Meco' breathing apparatus which had to be worn as the workings were full of fumes from the fire raging over 1,000 ft below.

ANOTHER GROUP OF RESCUERS with breathing apparatus inside the pit-head buildings. Note the large slope-sided chaldron wagons used to transport coal to the docks.

A POSTCARD, commemorating the Wellington Pit Disaster, the worst in Cumbria, which occurred in May 1910. A total of 136 men and boys were lost.

A MEMORIAL to victims of the 1910 disaster in St Begh's Roman Catholic church.

PART OF THE FUNERAL CORTEGE of some of the victims proceeds along Low Road to the cemetery.

SALTOM PIT. This badly faded photograph is believed to date from around 1860, and shows the remains of a very remarkable pit sunk on the sea shore between 1729 and 1731. It was the first major colliery to work below the sea and provided the samples of methane used to investigate the nature and properties of this gas. It was elliptical in section, and a vertical divider of baulks of timber ran from top to bottom along the short axis, forming a double shaft. This allowed a positive ventilation system to be used for the first time, air being sucked down one side of the shaft, and stale air containing mine gases ejected from the other by means of a furnace kept burning at the bottom of the 'up-cast' half. It is also said to be the first time that gunpowder was used to assist shaft sinking. Drainage water from many other pits situated on higher land was channelled into Saltom, where huge steam engines pumped the workings dry. This drainage system, and the pumps, were kept in use long after the coal workings at Saltom were abandoned. Some of the pit-head buildings have survived and are being restored as an industrial monument.

THE SINKING OF HAIG PIT, 1914. The last major pit to be sunk, and the last to close, Haig was commenced during the First World War and lasted until 1986. It was situated on high land close to the Wellington Pit and overlooking the site of Saltom. Temporary surface buildings surround the headgear used for sinking the shaft.

BUILDING THE ENGINE HOUSE AT HAIG PIT, 1916.

INSIDE THE ENGINE HOUSE, *c.* 1920. The massive steam-powered winding engines at Haig were among the finest installed in any British pit. They were actually built for a textile mill, but war-time priorities resulted in their being modified for use at Haig. Although the possibility of converting them to electric power had been considered, these magnificent engines continued to employ steam right up to the time of closure. The engine house and its contents remain, and it is hoped to preserve and restore these remains as an industrial museum.

PART OF THE LABORATORY AT HAIG PIT, *c.* 1920.

HAIG PIT DISASTER, SEPTEMBER 1922. This was the worst of several disasters at Haig, when thirty-nine men lost their lives. Note the three ambulances on the right.

THE SINKING OF LADYSMITH PIT, 1902. The new shaft of Ladysmith was sunk adjacent to Croft Pit, seen on the left. The wagons contain slabs of rock quarried nearby which were to be used for lining the shaft. This site is now covered by the chemical factory of Albright & Wilson.

COAL can be used to produce a vast range of by-products including gas, tar, creosote, dyes and many chemicals. A tar distillation plant was set up at Lowca, and this photograph, taken on 3 April 1924, shows the laying of some of its foundations.

THE SITE had been transformed by August 1924, creosote and crude tar storage tanks had already been installed.

'SELDOM SEEN' COTTAGE, GREENBANK, *c.* 1920. This cottage was the site of one of the scores of small-scale mines which were worked in this area. The Seldom Seen mine was one of the earliest, dating from the seventeenth century. The cottage was demolished in 1938.

COAL HORSES AT THE DOCKS, 1900. These horses were used to haul chaldron wagons along lines leading to various 'hurries' on the harbour side where collier vessels were loaded.

COAL PICKING AT SALTOM BROWS during the strike of 1912. The authorities turned a blind eye to people who helped themselves to coal picked from old spoil-heaps and workings when it was otherwise unavailable. The smoking chimney is at Haig Pit; the pumping engines had to be kept working even during a strike! West Pier is visible.

COAL PICKING AT SCILLY BANKS, Harras Moor during the 1926 General Strike. These workings, part of the Whingill colliery complex inland from Whitehaven, had been abandoned long before this period.

DUKE PIT FANHOUSE, *c.* 1970. This curious building housed a huge fan which was used to draw air from the workings of Duke Pit. The negative pressure so caused sucked air throughout the workings. This superseded the system known as 'coursing the air' by means of a furnace at the foot of the 'up-cast' shaft. The fanhouse was to have been demolished in the 1960s, but on exposing the circular chamber, work was stopped and the decision taken to preserve this interesting relic. Unfortunately, the fan itself had been removed at some earlier period, but the fanhouse itself serves as a reminder of Whitehaven's mining era.

THE STEEL MILL, invented by Carlisle Spedding of Whitehaven around 1730, was the first attempt to produce a safe working light for use in coal mines. A piece of flint was pressed against the hardened steel disc (on the right) while the handle (the wooden part is missing from this specimen) was turned. The gearing made the steel disc rotate at high speed, producing a stream of sparks which gave a glimmer of light, but no continuous flame. Although the risk of explosion was greatly reduced, it is known that the steel mill could, and did ignite the gas. Nevertheless, during almost a century, until it was superseded by the Davy, Geordie and other true safety lamps, this device must have saved countless lives throughout the British Isles. This specimen is displayed in Whitehaven Museum.

WOMEN SCREEN WORKERS in their canteen at William Pit, *c.* 1910.

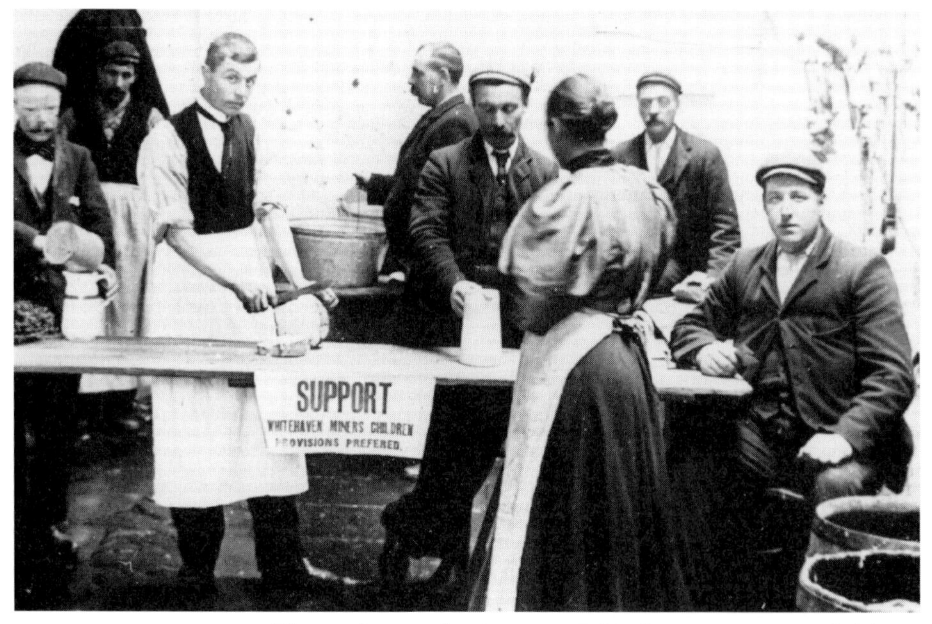

MINERS' SOUP KITCHEN. The notice reads 'Support Whitehaven Miners' Children. Provisions Preferred.' This was probably set up during the temporary closure of the Whitehaven pits in 1900.

SECTION FIVE

Iron Mining and Engineering

Iron ore of particularly fine quality is found in a zone around Maryport, through Grasmere to Kirby Lonsdale, from Lamplugh south to Egremont, and from Cleator Moor to Millom. In these areas ore was extracted, smelted and worked over a period of some 1,800 years. In 1711 the first blast furnace in Cumbria was erected at Backbarrow, in the south of the county, and others, using vast quantities of charcoal, were to follow. When Abraham. Darby of Coalbrookdale, Shropshire perfected smelting using coke for firing, a tremendous increase in iron production became possible, and during the nineteenth century scores of blast furnaces were installed in Cumberland. Thomas Bessemer's converter was one of the key inventions of the nineteenth century, permitting, for the first time, the large scale conversion of iron into the much stronger and more versatile material steel. His original method could not remove certain impurities from the iron, and he was compelled to undertake a survey of the world's major deposits of ore to find the purest available source. Eventually he discovered that haematite from Cumberland was the richest and purest of the hundreds of samples analysed. Accordingly, the first converters were set up near Barrow, which consequently became one of Britain's major builders of steel ships, particularly of battleships and, later, submarines.

The premium placed upon Cumberland iron ore led to a tremendous growth in iron mining, but the boom was not to last. By using specially formulated firebricks to line the converter, the impurities present in other ores could be removed. Consequently, huge quantities of relatively cheap ore were imported and the Cumbrian mines, which were in any case becoming worked out, started to close. Today only one haematite mine remains in production the 'Florence' at Egremont. This, the only working haematite mine in Europe, is becoming a tourist attraction in its own right.

The traditional local industries, coal and ironmining, steelmaking and ship building, required foundries and engineering workshops and many were established locally to produce machinery, chains and castings. The largest was a firm originally established as Heslop, Millward & Stead in 1799. Its name changed several times, Millward & Co. in 1808, Tulk & Ley in 1837, Fletcher Jennings in 1857, the Lowca Engineering Company in 1884, and the New Lowca Engineering Co. in 1905. A serious fire in 1912 destroyed a good deal of the premises and production ceased in 1921.

BLAST FURNACES of the Lonsdale Iron Works, Whitehaven, *c.* 1890. These were situated to the north of William Pit. They were not particularly successful as the pig-iron produced there was of poor quality. The company was liquidated in 1902 and was wound up in 1904.

INSTALLATION OF NEW BOILER at Lamplugh iron mine in 1911.

GENERAL VIEW of Lamplugh iron mine in October 1911.

MINING ACCIDENT at Townhead, near Egremont, 1913. Men were trapped some 75 ft below ground and part of the workings was flooded. A 3-in borehole was sunk to reach the men so that food could be lowered to them.

DIVERS GARSTANG AND BENSON dived through 75 ft of water to rescue the trapped men.

WEIGHBRIDGE, 1888. This is believed to have been taken at Crowgarth Mine No. 4, Cleator Moor. On the left of the group stands Mr Brayton Burrow, weighman.

ULLCOATS MINERS' STRIKE, 1907. The iron ore miners parading along Egremont's Main Street.

TOP OF SHAFT, HAILE MOOR IRON MINE, *c.* 1955. Note the small size of the tubs compared to those used in coal mining; iron ore is very much heavier.

AERIAL ROPEWAY, *c.* 1955. This was used to transport iron ore from the mine to a hopper, from which it was dropped directly into trucks on the railway line.

CLEATOR MOOR FORGE at Woodend, 1895. This forge, established in the mid-eighteenth century, was owned in 1895 by Messrs S. & J. Lindow, manufacturers of spades and shovels. They owned another forge at Bridgefoot, near Workington, and the company's office was in Albion Street, Whitehaven.

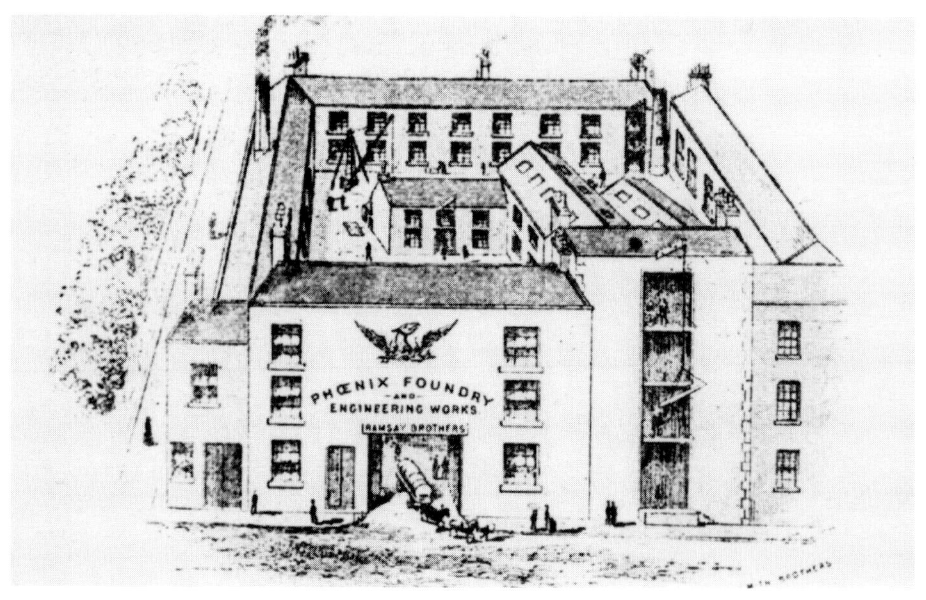

PHOENIX FOUNDRY AND ENGINEERING WORKS, Albion Street, Whitehaven, 1895. The business was established in 1866 by Messrs W. & T. Ramsay. This engraving appears to be the only picture of the premises.

A TRADE DISPLAY by Messrs Andrew McArd and Co., 'Engineers furnishers, Oil and Colourmen, Iron, Steel and Metal Merchants' of Williamson Lane, Whitehaven, 1895.

INSIDE MCARD'S WAREHOUSE, 1895.

PATENT PIG-IRON BREAKING MACHINE, designed and built at Lowca Engineering Co. *c.* 1910. The crane is lifting huge comb-shaped pieces of pig-iron from railway flat trucks on to the bed of the machine, where it will be smashed into fragments ready for converting into steel.

INTERIOR OF THE ROLLING MILL at Moss Bay Iron Works, Workington, *c.* 1900. The engines were almost certainly built by the Lowca Engineering Co.

SECTION SIX

The Railways

Transporting coal from pit-head to harbour was one of the biggest problems faced by the Lowthers. For decades, hundreds of pack horses and ponies were used to carry coal in panniers, but this was an extremely expensive and inefficient operation. In 1683 John Gale, the Lowther's steward, constructed a 'coal-way' known also as the Causey or Causeway, from Woodagreen Pit to the harbour. The track was made as level and regular as possible, then baulks of timber were laid on which the wheels of carts were run. As there were no flanges on the wheels or guiding bars on the track the driver had to steer the horse-drawn trucks down the incline. The causeway, although primitive, was very successful, greatly reducing transportation costs. Other, more advanced 'wooden railways' were constructed and later these were fitted with iron rails and flanged wheels. Such tracks, used in many collieries, were the forerunners of railways as we know them. The true steam-powered railway reached Whitehaven in 1847. This was an extension, known as the Whitehaven Junction Railway, of the Maryport Carlisle Line opened in stages between 1840 and 1845. The Whitehaven & Furness Junction Railway ran southwards from Whitehaven along the coast, via St Bees, to Millom and Barrow. This line was completed in 1850, but at that time there was no direct connection between the two. Passengers travelling north had to alight at Corkickle station to connect with a train destined for Carlisle. This problem was overcome two years later on completion of Bransty tunnel, which passes beneath much of the town. Meanwhile, a complex network of minor lines and mineral railways was being constructed to serve the towns and villages, iron and coal mines and quarries of the area. Sadly these have all been torn up, leaving only the Cumbrian coastal railway, one of the country's most scenic lines, and the miniature 15-in gauge Ravenglass & Eskdale Railway, one of the main tourist attractions of the region. The Lowca Engineering Company, mentioned in the previous section, produced about 260 locomotives – mainly sturdy tank engines used by local pits and mines. Later, the company specialized in the narrow gauge engines used in quarries. The famous *Baxter* of the Bluebell Railway was one of their products, and two others are still in use on the Talylyn Railway of North Wales. However, Lowca's most remarkable achievement was the construction of the first Crampton patent locomotives. T.R. Crampton (1816–88), who had been trained as a railway engineer on Brunel's Great Western Railway, devised a means of constructing locomotives of power equal to those used on the GWR's broad gauge railway for use on the narrower standard track. After many abortive attempts to interest well known locomotive builders in his revolutionary design, he eventually approached

THE MARCHON BRAKE , 1970. This photograph shows a 'passing loop', where trucks being hauled uphill were able to pass those going down. Over the rest of the track the middle rail was common to both tracks – a rather unusual feature. Reminiscent of the early 'inclined plane' causeways used for moving coal down the slope to the harbour, the brake was used for hauling phosphate rock to the works. It was in use until a few years ago.

Messrs Tulk and Ley of Lowca, who undertook the consrtuction of the first of these somewhat bizarre locomotives in 1846. *Namur* and *Liege*, the prototypes with 7 ft driving wheels were ordered for the Belgian Railway, and in Europe the design caused a sensation. For many years Crampton locomotives were the fastest expresses on the Continent. In all, the Lowca Company produced five of these locomotives, one of which was used on the Maryport and Carlisle Railway. Other British companies built Crampton locomotives but none has been preserved, although the *Fire Queen* at Penrhyn Castle, North Wales is very reminiscent of Crampton's designs. These locomotives did not prove popular in Britain but they were an important step in the development of standard gauge railways.

THE CREST OF THE WHITEHAVEN JUNCTION RAILWAY, *c.* 1855. This painted wooden panel in Whitehaven Museum was salvaged from the exterior of a door of a first-class carriage used on this line.

BRANSTY STATION, 1877. The approach to the station crowded with people, presumably about to board an excursion train. Note the voluminous skirts of several of the ladies and the gentleman in a top hat. The railings on the extreme right surrounded the Grand Hotel.

MAIN FAÇADE OF BRANSTY STATION, 1907. This building was large and opulent since it was the northern terminus of the Furness Railway. It housed a large board room that had previously been accommodated in the Railway Hotel which subsequently became the Grand Hotel on the station approach.

THE STATION SEEN FROM BRANSTY HILL, 1976. The very unusual triangular plan of the station buildings is clearly visible. Trains emerge from Bransty tunnel whose parapet is seen on the left. Beyond this is a group of buses, parked in what was formerly the railway carriage shed.

BRANSTY RAILWAY STATION, *c.* 1885. A similar view, showing the façade on the extreme right and shipyard on North Shore, and a panoramic view of the harbour and Wellington Pit on South Beach. The impressive station buildings have since been replaced by a neat modern building which, although adequate, has none of the glamour of its Victorian predecessor.

PRESTON STREET GOODS YARD, *c.* 1970. The marshalling yards and goods sheds were vitally important in Victorian times when Whitehaven was still a thriving industrial centre. These sheds give some indication of the scale of these operations.

AN 0–4–0 TANK LOCOMOTIVE, *c.* 1890. This engine, works number 161/1879 was built by Fletcher Jennings of Lowca and operated at Whitehaven between 1879 and 1895 when it was scrapped.

ABERNANT, *c.* 1880. This was built by Fletcher Jennings in 1867 (works number 65/1867). It was sold to the Abernant Iron Works, Glamorgan, hence its name.

A SADDLE TANK LOCOMOTIVE built by the Lowca Engineering Company, 1894.

MON DESERT, *c.* 1912. Built by the New Lowca Engineering Co., the engine is seen here after completion but before painting, in the assembly shed.

CRANE LOCOMOTIVE *SNIPY*, built 1890. This curious engine was built by Neilson and Co. of Glasgow and was used by the Hodbarrow Mining Company.

A 'SENTINEL' DIESEL, No. 10036, built in 1961. It was used as a demonstration locomotive until bought by the Marchon Chemical Company in 1962.

SECTION SEVEN

Other Places

LOWCA, PARTON AND MORESBY

THE FAMOUS LOWCA ENGINEERING WORKS, *c.* 1900. This long-established works was almost destroyed by fire in 1912. It struggled along for some years afterwards but was wound up in 1929. Lowca, Parton and Moresby are three small villages to the north of Whitehaven. Lowca is remembered chiefly as the home of the Lowca Engineering Company which operated under various names from 1799 to 1926. Parton was a port, but its development was deliberately suppressed by the Lowthers as it was taking some of the trade from Whitehaven. Moresby, the site of a small Roman fort, was the home of the Fletcher family of coal owners and has expanded greatly as a residential area in recent years.

MACHINE AND ERECTING SHOP at Lowca, 1895.

COGGING MILL MACHINERY installed by Lowca Engineering Co. at Moss Bay Haematite Iron & Steel Co. Ltd, Workington, 1891.

STEAM-POWERED ROAD CARRIAGE built at Lowca early in the First World War. This was submitted to the War Department in the hope of obtaining a contract, but was unsuccessful.

VIEW OF PARTON showing the railway lines which run alongside the coast.

COAL PICKERS on the beach at Parton during the 1921 strike.

FOUNDRY ROAD, PARTON, *c.* 1935.

CHILDREN ENJOYING A RIDE on the ash cart at Parton, *c.* 1905.

MORESBY HALL, photographed around 1870. This splendid old building incorporates an ancient piel tower.

ST BEES HEAD, *c.* 1885. Although sea-walls and groynes have been built, and the beach today is a popular tourist attraction, the scene has changed little in a century.

The parish of St Bees derives its name from the Irish saint Bega, who founded a nunnery here around AD 650. Several legends about St Bega survive, but there is virtually no reliable information about the development of the priory before Norman times when it was enlarged as a Benedictine Abbey. Various rights and parcels of land were granted to the Abbey, which continued to expand until the Dissolution of the Monasteries under Henry VIII. Eventually, the decaying remains of the old Abbey were refurbished to form the present Priory Church.

The sandstone cliffs of St Bees have become a major sanctuary for seabirds.

PRIORY CHURCH OF ST BEES, *c.* 1885.

INTERIOR OF THE CHURCH *c.* 1885. The church contains a magnificent organ, the last to be built under the personal supervision of 'Father' Willis, the best known British organ-builder. Installed in 1899, it occupies an entire transept of the church and is on the scale of a cathedral organ. It remains more or less unchanged in almost a century.

THE FINE NORMAN WEST DOOR OF THE CHURCH, *c.* 1885.

THE COURTYARD OF ST BEES SCHOOL, *c.* 1899. The public school at St Bees was founded in 1587 by Edmund Grindal, who was born in the village and not at Hensingham, as has been claimed, and who became Archbishop of Canterbury under Elizabeth I.

HEADMASTER'S HOUSE, ST BEES SCHOOL, *c.* 1885.

THESE COTTAGES, called Hygiene Place, still exist about a century later. The hooped skirt might suggest an earlier date, but the lady may have continued to wear this dress long after it had become unfashionable; it is dangerous to date a photograph on a single piece of circumstantial evidence!

THE REMAINS OF A STONE-BUILT CASTLE, erected between AD 1120 and 1270 stand atop a steep mound overlooking the little town of Egremont. This Norman stronghold was for generations the administrative headquarters of the barony of Kaupland (hence the modern name of the borough – Copeland). The town was established by the Normans in a clearing made in the great forest which then clothed much of the region. It was essentially a farming community but, later, iron mines, tanneries, flax mills and three paper mills were established there. These industries, with the exception of the 'Florence' ironmine, which is now the last working haematite mine in Europe, have long since disappeared. For almost 750 years the famous Crab Fair has been held at Egremont. This perpetuates the granting of a Market Charter to the town by Henry III, and it takes place on the Saturday nearest to 19 September. The festivities include 'gurning' in which contestants compete to pull the most grotesque face through a horse collar! The postcard shows the castle gateway about 1905.

CRAB FAIR SPORTS.

THE Ancient and Annual SPORTS, at EGRE-
MONT will be held an SATURDAY the 18th of Sep-
ember, 1824, when the following Prizes will be given to
ontend for :—

A handsome SILVER CUP, of Two Guineas value, to
Vrestle for, which will be given to the last Stander, and small-
r Prizes for the second, third, and fourth.

Mr LITT, (Author of Wrestliana) Umpire.

HALF A GUINEA to Quoit for;—a good HAT to b
Run for by Men; and a PAIR OF GLOVES to Leap for,
&c. &c.

N. B. The Stewards will be on the Ground at Half past
Three o'Clock in the Afternoon, to enter Names for the
Vresling, which will commence at Four.

All Disputes to be settled by the Stewards, or whom they
ay appoint.

JONATHAN BOADLE, }
JOHN SEWELL, } Stewards.

Egremont, 4 September, 1824.

ADVERTISEMENT from the *Cumberland Pacquet* newspaper, 6 September 1824.

EGREMONT CASTLE GROUNDS, *c*. 1905. Such a clear view of the castle is impossible today as tall trees now obscure the slopes of the mound.

CASTLE GARDENS, *c.* 1920. Sadly such lavish floral displays can no longer be provided.

MARKET PLACE, *c.* 1905. The central feature is a drinking-water fountain which was unveiled by Mr Muncaster, a local bank manager, on 23 November 1904.

MARKET PLACE, *c.* 1925. Note the memorial to men lost in the First World War and, on the left, the long arm of a petrol pump extending high above the pavement to serve the second car.

EGREMONT BAND poses before parading to celebrate the unveiling of the war memorial.

EGREMONT'S FIRE ENGINE, *c.* 1920.

BALLOON ASCENT AT EGREMONT. This was scheduled to take place on 22 June 1911 to mark the coronation of George V, but was postponed until the next day due to bad weather. The balloon, filled with gas from Egremont gas works, seen in the background, was 36 ft in diameter. Captain Spencer allowed it to rise to 3,000 ft, then parachuted down to land on the football field.

THE MARKET SQUARE, Cleator Moor from a postcard of about 1925. Although Cleator itself is of considerable antiquity, the adjoining town of Cleator Moor was created during the nineteenth century to house the many hundreds of miners who flooded into the area, largely from Ireland, to develop the haematite mines. Of these mines, the 'Montreal', owned by J. Stirling, was the most important, having six shafts, one of which yielded coal as well as haematite. In 1842 an extensive range of blast furnaces was erected to produce pig-iron from the ore, and S. & J. Lindow's forge produced vast quantities of spades, shovels and other tools used in local mines. The huge flax mill of Ainsworth & Sons once employed over 600 workers and produced fine linen thread. It still stands but is now divided into small factory units. The iron ore mines, blast furnaces and spade forge have long since disappeared.

CLEATOR MOOR TOWN HALL, *c.* 1900. These attractive yet unpretentious buildings were erected in 1877 at a cost of £3,265.

McLEANS SHIPPING AGENCY, *c.* 1910. A considerable number of experienced iron ore miners emigrated from Cleator Moor, particularly to South Africa. Most of them made their travelling arrangements at this agency.

THE IRON WORKS OF THE WHITEHAVEN IRON AND STEEL COMPANY, 1910.

THE WORKERS AT HEATHCOTE'S FOUNDRY, *c.* 1900. Mr Heathcote himself stands on the extreme left of the middle row.

AINSWORTH'S LINEN THREAD MILL, *c.* 1900.

ST JOHN'S TEMPERANCE BAND, 1909.

GOSFORTH VILLAGE from a postcard of about 1905. The delightful village of Gosforth lies six miles south of Egremont and five miles north of Ravenglass.

THIS VERY FADED PHOTOGRAPH OF GOSFORTH CHURCH was taken in 1858, just before the ancient building was enlarged. Although the church now looks much like any other late Victorian reconstruction, it contains the most important collection of Viking carvings in the county. These include two spectacular 'hog-back' tombstones found during the 1896 rebuilding. These and other carvings are now preserved within the church.

THE RE-OPENING OF THE CHURCH, 1858. It was extensively rebuilt again in 1896.

GOSFORTH'S MOST FAMOUS FEATURE is the 14 ft high sandstone cross in the churchyard. It is the tallest cross of its kind in Britain, and dates from the sixth or seventh century. The railings in this magic lantern slide of about 1880 have since been removed.

REMAINS OF THE ROMAN BATH-HOUSE, Ravenglass, *c.* 1910. Not far away is the fort of Hardknott which was a considerable garrison overlooking the Solway. Hardknott Pass, a highly convoluted Roman road, leads to Ambleside, but extreme care must be exercised by motorists using it! Ravenglass village boasts many attractions: Roman remains, the famous 'Ratty' miniature railway, a working water-powered corn mill and, nearby, the superb Muncaster Castle with its extensive grounds featuring a huge collection of rhododendrons. Ravenglass lies at the confluence of three small rivers, the Mite, Irt and Esk, and its harbour, once used by the Romans, is now heavily silted.

RAVENGLASS VILLAGE is prone to flooding, as shown by this photograph of Main Street in 1915.

RAVENGLASS PARISH HALL BUILDINGS, erected in 1894, in a postcard of about 1905.

THE NEWTON BEACON. This was built as a navigational landmark in 1824 and photographed about a century later. It was demolished in the late 1930s.

MUNCASTER MILL, *c.* 1900. This water-powered corn mill has been fully restored and forms a tourist attraction beside the 'Ratty' miniature railway.

THE RAVENGLASS & ESKDALE RAILWAY, familiarly known as 'La'al Ratty' was built as a 3 ft gauge mineral line for haematite, but later became a passenger line. The 0–6–0 tank locomotive seen here in about 1900 was built by Manning Wardle in 1875.

THE 'RATTY' became a 15 in gauge railway in 1915. *Ella*, seen drawing the Bank Holiday Special at the old Ravenglass station in 1923, was scrapped three years later.

HOLY TRINITY CHURCH AND MILLOM CASTLE, *c.* 1905. Although originally a Norman structure, Holy Trinity Church was ruined architecturally in Victorian times by insensitive 'modernization' but some of its original features remain.

Until local government boundaries were revised in 1974, and part of northern Lancashire was incorporated into Cumbria, Millom stood at the southern limit of Cumberland. It now marks the lower boundary of the Borough of Copeland. Although not open to the public, Millom Castle still stands and is, in fact, still occupied. For centuries it was the home of the Lords of Millom, who governed the tip of Cumberland under a grant made by the Baron of Egremont. Its market charter was granted in 1250. Although iron was smelted from local ore from the late seventeenth century, Millom developed very little until the mid-nineteenth century when the huge iron ore deposits at Hodbarrow began to be exploited. Its harbour was then enlarged and a huge sea-wall a mile and a quarter in length was erected to protect the Hodbarrow mines, from which hundreds of thousands of tons of ore were extracted annually. The mine and its ancillary buildings closed many years ago and the harbour, once crowded with iron ore vessels, is used by a few pleasure boats.

MILLOM MARKET SQUARE, *c.* 1900. The council office building with its domed clock tower was built in 1880 at a cost of £4,000.

BLAST FURNACE, of the Millom and Askham Haematite Iron Company, *c.* 1890. Note the heaps of pig-iron, some of which is being transported on horse-drawn bogies.

CONSTRUCTION OF THE SEA-WALL, *c.* 1900. Note the massive masonry blocks being positioned on the parapet.

HULK OF A SAILING VESSEL at the river mouth about 1900.

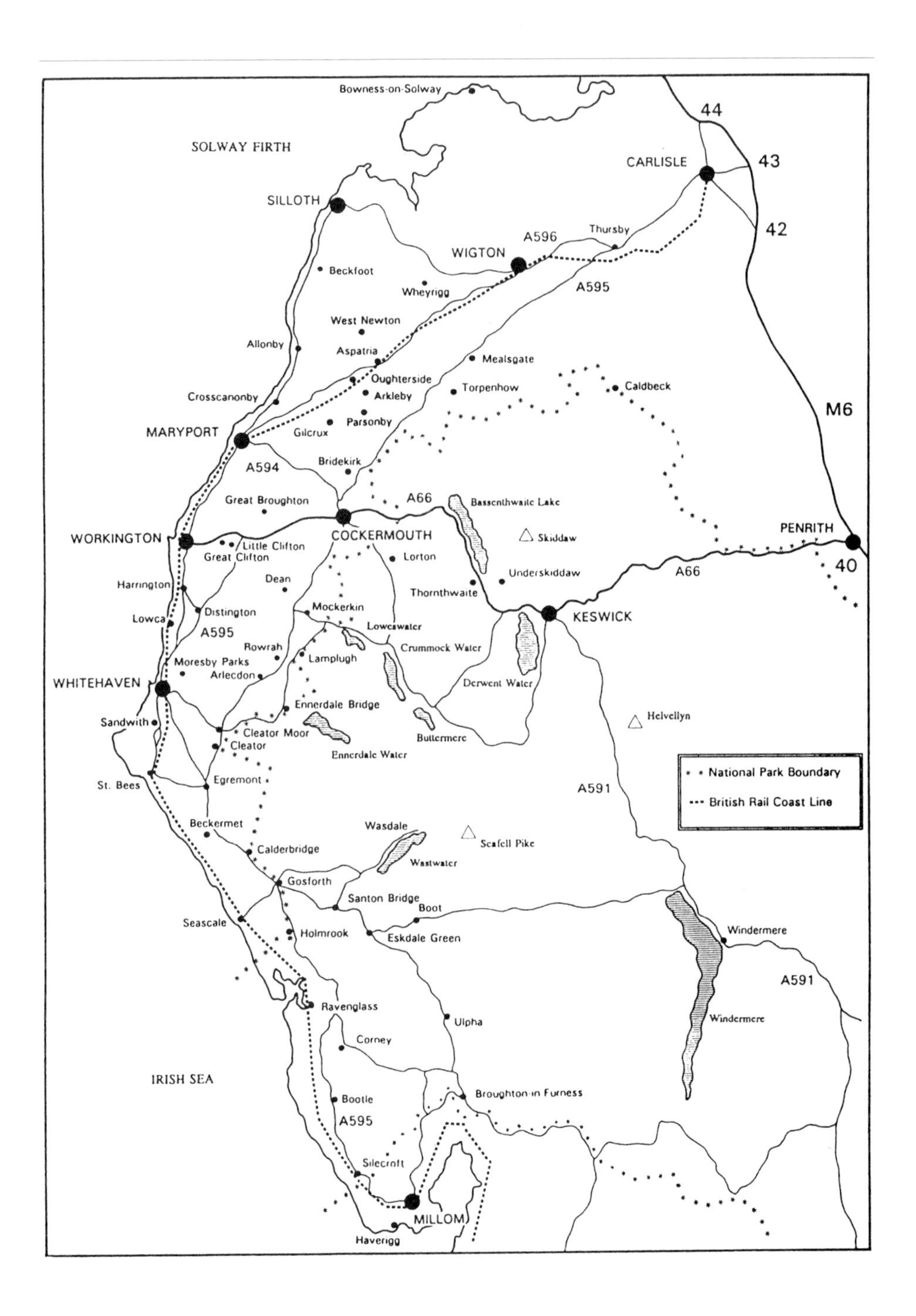
Bowness-on-Solway
SOLWAY FIRTH
44
CARLISLE
43
SILLOTH
42
Thursby
A596
WIGTON
Beckfoot
Wheyrigg
A595
West Newton
Allonby
Aspatria
Mealsgate
Oughterside
Arkleby
Torpenhow
Caldbeck
Crosscanonby
Parsonby
M6
MARYPORT
Gilcrux
A594
Bridekirk
Great Broughton
A66
Bassenthwaite Lake
COCKERMOUTH
Skiddaw
PENRITH
WORKINGTON
Little Clifton
Great Clifton
Lorton
40
Harrington
Dean
Underskiddaw
A66
Thornthwaite
Distington
Mockerkin
KESWICK
Lowca
Loweswater
A595
Crummock Water
Rowrah
Moresby Parks
Lamplugh
Arlecdon
WHITEHAVEN
Derwent Water
Ennerdale Bridge
Helvellyn
Sandwith
Cleator Moor
Buttermere
Cleator
Ennerdale Water
National Park Boundary
British Rail Coast Line
St. Bees
Egremont
A591
Beckermet
Wasdale
Scafell Pike
Calderbridge
Wastwater
Gosforth
Santon Bridge
Boot
Seascale
Windermere
Holmrook
Eskdale Green
A591
Ravenglass
Ulpha
Windermere
Corney
IRISH SEA
Broughton-in Furness
Bootle
A595
Silecroft
MILLOM
Haverigg

AUTHOR'S NOTE AND ACKNOWLEDGEMENTS

Although Whitehaven's present museum was established in 1975, it was originally set up as a private museum by members of the Whitehaven Scientific Society over a century earlier. Unfortunately, this worthy organization was wound up after the First World War, and its collections were deposited with the town's public library. During the 1950s an extension to the library premises was desperately needed, and the museum building was demolished to provide the site. Consequently much of the collection was disposedof, the residue being stored in boxes and parcels in every available nook and corner of the library.With the reorganization of local government in 1974, Copeland Borough Council came into being and it was decided that the town's museum should be resurrected, using the surviving specimens as the nucleus of its collection. On my appointment as the first curator of the 'New' Museum I was delighted to discover that the collection included a substantial number of photographs, magic lantern slides, and other illustrations of the area. Particularly significant among these is a group os about 200 lantern slides used by the late William Watson when giving lectures on the history of the town. These include many of the earliest views shown in this book. We have attempted to build on this firm foundation, and the museum's photographic survey of Copeland now comprises some 5,000 negatives. Although many of these were taken by museum staff and otphers to record recent changes and developments, the bulk have been copied from earlier phtographs kindly loaned by public-spirited individuals far too numerous to list. On behalf of the museum I do wish to thank the many people who have allowed us to copy such photographs; without their cooperation this book could not have been produced. Particular thanks must be given to Cliff Turner, a member of our very active 'Friends of the Museum' society, who for many years has produced prints from our collection including all those seen in this book, and Karl Wilson and to Val Hepworth who, thankfully gifted with second sight, 'translated' my virtually indecipherable scrawl to produce a computer print-out of the text. My sincere thanks must go also to Simon Thraves of Alan Sutton Publishing, who invited me to compile *Whitehaven in Old Photographs* and bore my procrastination with understanding and good humour. This book is a tribute to scores of people who have contributed to our collections or provided information about the history of the region. I hope it will encourage visitors to explore this remarkable and little known area which lies between the mountains of the Lake District and the Solway.